'A wide-ranging, thoughtful a
of areas of dissonance that ma
experience and creative insigh
embracing the tensions these c
Stuart Murray-Williams, author, Post-Christendom

'Trevor Neill is one of the most gifted pastor-theologians that we have. In this book he discusses the great issues facing the church. Trevor analyses our individualism, the cult of celebrity, our obsession with fads, the shallowness of much of our engagement with the world and our related complicity with power. He understands these things too well to offer any easy answers but instead points to ways forward that, if they form a consistent part of our practice, will actually address the things that are really going on. Trevor calls the church to true discipleship, to deep engagement in prayer, to the practice of lament, to mentoring and to social engagement based on reciprocity. The discussion questions after each chapter help make this a fine book for both personal and for group study for those who want to think deeply about church and society today.'
Steve Finamore, Principal, Bristol Baptist College

Bridging the Gaps

Identifying and overcoming the church's hidden divisions

Trevor Neill

instant
ap☐stle

First published in Great Britain in 2020

Instant Apostle

The Barn
1 Watford House Lane
Watford
Herts
WD17 1BJ

if notified, will formally seek permission at the earliest opportunity.

The views and opinions expressed in this work are those of the author and do not necessarily reflect the views and opinions of the publisher.

British Library Cataloguing-in-Publication Data

A catalogue record for this book is available from the British Library.

This book and all other Instant Apostle books are available from Instant Apostle:

Website: www.instantapostle.com

E-mail: info@instantapostle.com

ISBN 978-1-912726-15-8

Printed in Great Britain.

Contents

Acknowledgements

An old proverb reminds us that it takes a village to raise a child, and likewise it could be said that it takes a church to write a book. For all the blessings of academia, the local congregation, a community of people, some of whom are new to faith, others mature or clinging on, where babies are being dedicated, converts baptised, and the faithful given thanks for, is undoubtedly the best place to do theology. This book is written with a debt of thanks to all of the churches I've been part of, but especially those I've had the privilege to serve as pastor: Yardley Wood Baptist Church, who generously supported me through Master's studies; and Selsdon Baptist Church, who made time available to me to complete the final version of this book.

I am also grateful to the many friends and conversation partners who have provided an inspiration and example, encouraging and helping me to reflect on the issues covered in this book, and many more besides: Alan Pain, Andy Flannagan, Andy Delmege, Colin Neill, Fernando de Paula, Tim Pearson, Steve Finamore, Tim Fergusson, Ken Stewart, Mike Pears, and Stuart and Sian Murray-Williams.

My thanks also to Nicki Copeland and the team at Instant Apostle, for all their support, wisdom and encouragement through the publication process.

Finally, the biggest thanks of all must go to Emma, James and Hannah. How to express my gratitude to them and for them, for putting up with all the hours spent with 'the book', for believing in it at the times when I didn't, and for all the love, insights and support given along the way?

Foreword
Andy Flannagan, singer-songwriter and Executive Director of Christians in Politics

I first got to know the writing of Trevor Neill when we were both aged 14. Let me paint a picture for you. I sit in the bedroom he shares with his twin brother Colin. We are surrounded by hundreds of past issues of *Autocar* magazine stacked up against their bunk beds, hidden under all manner of West Ham paraphernalia. Trevor is reading me the first chapter of the novel he and Colin have written. It is the founding document of the Anti-Rugby Society (work that out for yourself) of Portadown College. Our school had a proud heritage of playing rugby, but Trev and some others were playfully calling it out as the idol it sometimes was, though no one had previously had the nerve to say it.

Even at that age, Trev was keen to question accepted wisdom and seek perspective on the culture he found himself in. This book represents the continuation of that search. It is rare to find such humility, honesty and boldness from the pen of someone who is still in the midst of the everyday of pastoring people.

I think the most important thing for me to say in this foreword is that Trevor Neill is the real deal. I'll do that instead of rehashing his arguments here, because, as ever, Trev makes the case more eloquently than I could. This piece of meticulous research and testimony sits happily within the rest of Trev's world. The thoughtful, loving human being he has always been screams out of each page. This is not a piece of academic work separate from the people he has given himself to over three decades. The love of the underdog (first shown through his dedicated following of West Ham) is there. His ability to sniff out worrying trends in culture before they fully arrive is there. His ability to love the church and at the same time critique it is there. In fact, that old cliché that God loves us just as we are but loves us too much to leave us that way, applies well to Trevor's attitude to the bride of Christ.

Poems. So many poems. As a teenager and student, Trev was a prolific producer of poetry that was both insightful and powerful. I often sang his parody of Billy Joel's 'Piano Man' and it never failed to produce mirth and sombre reflection in equal measure. Nearly thirty years later I can still recall most of the words – for example:

Now the church bells sound like a death knell
And the prophets' pleas are ignored.
And it's only each other we're coming to see
'Cos we don't want to meet with the Lord.

Even then he was applying his God-given intellect, wit and heart to the Presbyterian context he found himself in. Those same attributes shine out of this book, now blessed with decades of experience, thus enabling him to see from both sides the generation gap he describes so accurately in chapter 6.

Trev is a wonderful father, a loyal friend and someone who has chosen the hard yards of serving the least, the last and the lost. Contained in these pages is the hard-won wisdom of someone who has seen life through the eyes of those who presently don't tend to come anywhere near churches. There are stories of those left behind in once-industrial heartlands, those who are victims of an increasingly atomised society and those who will never follow a purely cerebral religion.

It is not surprising that Trev has produced a book that is much deeper in its understanding of real people than many of its contemporaries. This is because he has been a pioneer in forms of communication that are fit for the twenty-first century. For example, he has inspired people with the boldness of dialogue-based preaching, allowing conversations to happen that lead to greater understanding and actual behavioural change in a community. He has had the nerve to hand the microphone to other people, and in this book I really think you can hear their voices.

As I have read this book, my wife has been regularly disturbed by my shouts of, 'This is brilliant!' You know those moments when someone expresses what you feel in your guts but does it in a hugely more articulate and evidenced way than you could? It was a regular experience for me throughout this book, which will leave the reader not just convinced of Trev's arguments but also better informed to make those arguments elsewhere.

Trevor's passion for the primacy of the local places he has served in church leadership shines through in every chapter. I especially enjoyed his forensic examination of a new generation who forsake the benefit of engaging with elders in their local area in favour of listening to podcasts from further afield. The warning about the danger of the increasing gap between the place where someone learns and where they serve is particularly potent. His heart is that mission and discipleship be woven together as it was for the very first disciples. It is just one example of Trev's refreshing honesty in analysing how the tides of culture inevitably affect all of us.

So please read this book. I guess if you are reading this foreword, it's a good start. The book is significant. It is potent. You will end up quoting large chunks of it to your small group, to your church leadership team or even to other people on the bus.

Most importantly, however, my prayer is that you yourself will experience an impartation of rifle-like wisdom and shotgun-like love from it, as I have done.

Bless you.

Introduction

Sermons go to work on us in strange, almost inexpressible, ways. Sometimes, what we recall years after the event are not specific words or illustrations, or even the identity of the speaker. Instead, what lingers is an impression made upon us, a feeling of conviction or excitement which remains even if the detail of what was said has not stayed in our long-term memory.

One such event happened for me in the late 1990s, the address delivered in the closing celebration service of a major evangelical festival, when the faithful were offered 'one for the road', a last shot of energy and inspiration to take with them to the churches and contexts of daily life. I can still recall a sense of tangible expectancy, which we were experiencing in more ways than one. My wife was pregnant with our first child, and had felt him kicking in her womb for the first time during one of the week's evening celebrations, responding to the atmosphere of worship which surrounded him, moving as if in the spirit of the unborn John the Baptist who sensed the presence of his Lord as Elizabeth and Mary greeted each other. Expectation levels were raised as well by the preacher, who confidently predicted that each one of us would be returning not to more of the same, but to a new season of revival when a rain of blessing would fall, bringing new and abundant life to people and churches which were dry and parched.

Even at the time I felt a certain detachment and wariness about what was being said. I remember how the thought came to me that this could be the ecclesiastical equivalent of David Steel's famous speech at the end of the 1981 Liberal Party Conference, when he famously told activists to, 'Go back to your constituencies and prepare for government.'[1] I wondered how such bullish predictions of church growth would stand the test of time, how energised we would all be a few months down the line when we were no longer fuelled by the high-octane mix on offer in the Big Top.

Perhaps my wariness was founded on a sense of having heard such sermons on a recurring basis during the 1990s. This was the era of Toronto, when evangelicals laughed and toppled as the Spirit moved in worship, and the 'Decade of Evangelism', when we took to the streets to march for Jesus and proclaimed His message with boldness and confidence. Another abiding memory from the same period is of joining thousands of other Christians in Wembley Arena to sing of Jesus as 'Champion of the World'. Our own church, planted like so many others in the 1990s and comprising mainly young families, had experienced some growth but nothing which quite matched the language of our worship.

I wonder how other evangelicals of my generation feel as they look back on the bombastic confidence of the 1990s. Today, the signs outside our local churches are as likely to advertise a foodbank or a debt counselling service as

Alpha or Christianity Explored. Somewhere along the way we rediscovered our social conscience. In part, we did so in a rush to fill a space vacated by the state, as the word 'austerity' became part of our everyday lexicon with the arrival of the coalition government of 2010, though I wonder if the changing emphases in our church programmes reflect a ruefulness about previous forms of evangelism which focused on words and proclamation at the expense of practical action. Could it also be the case that we speak fewer words because we're no longer sure of what to say? Old certainties on topics such as sexuality and heaven and hell have been displaced by an awareness of how shrill and unwelcoming we've sounded in the past, an appreciation of the need to allow doubt to be expressed and the importance of listening with greater openness to people who have previously felt pushed away.

It was the psychologist Leon Festinger who first used the term 'cognitive dissonance' to describe the stress we experience when trying to hold in tension contradictory beliefs and behaviour in our lives.[2] For example, we loathe ourselves because we continue to smoke in spite of our knowledge of the harm we're doing to our bodies, or we continue to drive a petrol-guzzling car even though to do so is at odds with a genuine concern we feel for the environment. Ultimately, the only way to overcome such problems is to either modify our practice or our attitude.

As I reflect on my own experiences of church leadership and have spoken with others in similar positions, it has occurred to me that many of us might be living with stresses, doubts that won't go away or a discontent with the status quo, which are best explained by Festinger's theory. There are gaps between the ways we live and the things we believe. Our churches increasingly invest their time in projects that demonstrate the values of the kingdom but much of our theology continues to be shaped by an understanding of the gospel that focuses on saving the world one individual at a time. Sunday by Sunday, we sing of our trust in God and His providence, but during the week we exhaust ourselves with increasingly busy programmes of activity as we search desperately for the silver bullet which will bring the church growth we hope to see. And our songs of unwavering trust and confidence in God can sometimes feel disconnected from lives in which we are experiencing the same battles with doubt or anxiety as everyone else.

In his letter to early Christian believers, James makes no reference to cognitive dissonance. But he did encourage those looking for wisdom to '... ask in faith, never doubting, for the one who doubts is like a wave of the sea, driven and tossed by the wind' (James 1:6, NRSV).

The ocean waves which lap upon our shores are caused by the pull of two opposing forces, the gravitational pull of the sun and that of the moon. It's stressful and exhausting to constantly be pulled in different directions, in contrast to the peace which James later describes as a hallmark of the lives of those who are 'wise and understanding' (James 3:13-18).

Often, the first and most important step in solving a problem is to acknowledge its existence. *Bridging the Gaps* has been written in an attempt to articulate and help us understand some of the tensions our churches are going through, the complications and contradictions we need to acknowledge so that we can grow and know a peace-giving convergence between what we believe and life as we experience it.

Notes

[1] See http://news.bbc.co.uk/1/hi/uk_politics/3185313.stm (accessed 28th July 2019).
[2] See https://www.simplypsychology.org/cognitive-dissonance.html (accessed 28th July 2019).

Chapter One
The Gap between Individualism
and Community

In March 1845, a group of around 100 young men in Leeds gathered together at one of the mutual societies which were commonplace at the time, organisations which enabled their working-class members to support each other in the quest for self-improvement. We have no record of the impression made upon that audience, but what we do know is that the event proved to be seminal for the speaker, a turning point in the career of one of the most prominent public figures in Victorian England.[1]

Samuel Smiles had a Reformed Presbyterian upbringing in his native Scotland and initially pursued a career in medicine. He had moved away from the faith of his youth and become a journalist by the time he'd settled in Leeds in 1838 and spent the next ten years campaigning with many others for causes such as the extension of suffrage and better education for the working classes. In his March 1845 talk, he encouraged his listeners to see self-improvement as more than a means by which their own circumstances might be improved. Instead, he said:

> The grand object aimed at should be to make the great mass of the people virtuous, intelligent, well-informed, and well-conducted; and to open to them new sources of pleasure and happiness. Knowledge is of itself one of the higher enjoyments.[2]

So began a new chapter in the life of the man regarded as Britain's first self-help guru. Smiles returned to give further talks to Leeds' aspiring young workers, lectures which inspired the material for his most famous work, *Self-Help*, published in 1859. Few of us today may have heard of Smiles, but it's almost impossible to overstate his significance to Victorians which can be best understood by considering some remarkable statistics about his literary output. Within a year of its release, 20,000 copies of *Self-Help* had been sold, and, by the time of his death in 1904, 258,000 had been bought by British readers. *Self-Help* outsold every novel of the nineteenth century and was translated into numerous other languages, including eighteen editions and 75,000 copies sold in Italian. Dominic Sandbrook notes, 'At Wormwood Scrubs, *Self-Help* was reportedly the most popular title in the prison library'.[3] A number of other books followed, including *Character* (1871), *Thrift* (1875) and *Duty* (1887).

Samuel Smiles wasn't the only Victorian figure to emphasise the importance of personal responsibility and self-discipline. We can't even be sure that he was the inventor of the term 'self-help', which others attribute to his contemporary, Thomas Carlyle.[4] It's also worth noting that the book is not a celebration of self-advancement for its own sake, emphasising the importance of other values such as honesty and good character.

And yet there's no doubt that Samuel Smiles' books captured perfectly the mood of his time, an insistence on the potential each person had to improve their lot in life through commitment and hard work. This was also the period when the wealth of the Industrial Revolution was beginning to be shared by the new and emerging middle class, people who for the first time could put distance between themselves and those beneath them by buying goods and a lifestyle which put their new wealth on display.[5] And it's no coincidence that this era also saw the emergence of a new and significant force in the church, the evangelicals.

'A personal Jesus': the rise of the evangelicals

When we try to understand the stories of the generations who came before us, one of our biggest potential problems is overcoming the temptation to assume that they saw the world in the same way we do, that their thinking, feeling and reacting was driven by impulses and presumptions which we regard as givens.

Most of us who have grown up in Britain in the late twentieth or early twenty-first centuries will take for granted the view that religion is a matter of individual choice. This perspective is one which will be reinforced for us if we attend an evangelical church, where we are regularly reminded that faith is not just about attendance at meetings or intellectual beliefs but also to do with our emotions, a love for God which is experienced as much in the heart as the head. Our worship songs and our teaching include a constant focus on our personal relationships with God, how to get close to Him, how to stay close and how to keep our love for Him alive. But it wasn't always so.

One of the best-known definitions of evangelicalism has been produced by the British historian David Bebbington, who identifies four hallmarks of evangelical belief and practice: biblicism (an emphasis on the authority of Scripture), activism (it's not just what we believe, living it out matters as well), crucicentrism (the central importance attached to the death of Jesus on the cross) and conversionism, 'the belief that lives need to be changed'.[6] But it's hard to understand the significance of this emphasis on individual experience without thinking more about the wider religious and social changes which took place as the evangelical movement emerged.

Most of us are probably familiar with the experience of going to church and then asking ourselves, perhaps on the way home or over Sunday lunch, 'how it was for us'. If we do analyse church in this way, there will probably be a number of factors which we take into consideration. Did we enjoy the worship and feel God's presence among us? Was there a sense of connectedness to God, for us personally and those around us? How was the sermon? It's not unreasonable that we ask ourselves these questions. Far better, most of us would agree, to think about and reflect on the extent to which we have properly engaged with God and the people of God, rather than just going through the motions.

However, questions such as these might never have occurred to previous generations of Christian worshippers. It's not that they didn't believe with the same intensity and devotion as us, people who might regard ourselves as more self-aware and attuned to our feelings. Those attending church through the Reformation and in the period following it understood the importance of salvation by faith alone, but did so with a confidence and assurance about how God can work through the faithful preaching of Scripture and celebration of sacraments, and in a time when how we *felt* at any given moment about all of this simply wasn't as important as it is now.[7]

All this changed, however, in the course of the Great Awakenings of the eighteenth and nineteenth centuries. It's been said that it was the eighteenth-century American revivalist preacher and theologian Jonathan Edwards who:

> made the crucial change when he developed a keen interest in the morphology of conversion, and when he decided to locate true religion in the affections.[8]

Such a perspective is probably taken for granted by many of us, but at the time the change it represented was dramatic. Now, the extent to which a person experienced an emotional quickening became the key measurement of the sincerity of their response to the gospel and, for later revivalists, it wasn't enough that such feelings were generated at the moment of conversion. The methods of Charles Finney provide an example of this approach:

> Find the most useful methods, ('excitements,' he called them) and there will be conversion. 'A revival will decline and cease,' he warned, 'unless Christians are frequently re-converted.'[9]

By the early nineteenth century, reports of revivalism were reaching England. Methodists, inspired by what they perceived as similarities between American camp meetings and the itinerant preaching of the Wesleys, decided to organise gatherings along similar lines. Later in the same century, D L Moody visited the United Kingdom, pioneering a new style of mass evangelism that relied on a combination of informal, conversational preaching and personal testimony, and gospel songs, most famously those of Ira Sankey, which invited an audience to express its response with the deeper sense of emotion generated by music.

It wasn't just the revivalists who contributed to the emergence of this new, confident and activist movement within the church. In 1846 the first meeting of the Evangelical Alliance had been held in London, attended by a variety of groups motivated by a greater desire for unity and the realisation of what might be achieved by working together on issues such as religious liberty.[10] This period also witnessed the increasing growth and confidence of the Nonconformists, churches whose model of worship emphasised the importance of the sermon and who produced a new generation of outstanding preachers, the most famous probably being the Baptist C H Spurgeon, who needed theatres and music halls to accommodate the crowds who flocked to hear him before the 5,000-seat Metropolitan Tabernacle was built in 1861. Meanwhile, in 1875 the first Keswick Convention was held, so establishing an important new fixture in the calendar of British evangelicalism.

When we look back at this period of evangelical history, it's important to recognise that this was not a generation preoccupied only with saving souls and cultivating personal devotion to God. As we'll discover later, the nineteenth century was also a period when many churches invested considerable resources in attempts to meet the physical needs of the poorest members of their community, with projects that included Sunday schools, household visiting and nursing, models of care and support which were the forerunners of our present health visiting and social work. However, it's hard to escape the impression that the evangelicals, especially those of the Free Churches, were developing a spirituality that encouraged a preoccupation firstly with one's own soul and secondly with the maintenance of increasingly busy programmes that made up local church life.

It's been noted that the book which best summed up the mindset of the Free Churchmen was Bunyan's *The Pilgrim's Progress*, the story of one believer's personal journey, enduring the trials and temptations of the world and eventually arriving unscathed in the Celestial City.[11] It's understandable that a sort of siege mentality must have been felt by people who still faced considerable barriers to their participation in wider society. It wasn't until 1854 and 1856, for example, that the removal of matriculation and graduation tests enabled Nonconformists to attend Oxford and Cambridge.[12] Yet there were other reasons for the distance they kept from those around them; a stress on the need for moral witness and a consciousness of dangers such as alcohol combined with social lives that revolved entirely around the activities of the chapel, creating a kind of holy disengagement from the world that was lived out by many Nonconformists.

There is much to be learned about the lives of the evangelicals by examining their spiritual perspectives. But one more factor needs to be considered if we're to fully understand this formative period in their history. Evangelicals weren't just experiencing church growth, they were also moving up in the world. They were getting richer.

In part, such social mobility can be explained by the ways in which chapels and churches developed qualities which enabled evangelicals to prosper in the world. The self-discipline which fostered spiritual growth went hand in hand with the hard work and determination needed to progress in the workplace, while the skills needed to organise the church meetings required by congregational government were similar to those which offered success in commerce or industry. The Reform Acts of 1867 and 1884 also opened up new opportunities for those attending the Free Churches.

Some church leaders recognised the potential risks associated with this increased prosperity, and the finery which came along with it. Commenting on the new habit of some Baptist ministers of wearing clerical collars and coats,[13] Spurgeon complained:

> Our working class will never be brought even to consider the truth of Christianity by teachers who are starched and fine.[14]

His comments were prescient: the late nineteenth and early twentieth centuries proved to be a high watermark for Nonconformists, who found themselves 'increasingly distanced … in ethos, worship and outlook from the working classes',[15] but enjoying a new-found prestige in society.

Of course, Nonconformists and evangelicals weren't the only group of people to benefit from the increased prosperity of the Victorian and Edwardian eras. In the same period, the Catholic Church sought to improve the quality of its schools, understanding education and an encouragement of sobriety and self-discipline to be means of changing the circumstances of its members, especially a wave of immigrants from Ireland.[16] But it seems to me that there was a particular set of influences which combined in this period to create a collective mindset still shared today by many evangelicals.

Consider the recipe: we take a belief in self-help and hard work which encourages people to apply themselves with discipline and determination to improving their circumstances in life. Remember Samuel Smiles? I wonder how many of those evangelicals who were making their way in the world in the Victorian era had a copy of *Self-Help* on their shelves. Add to that an increasing number of people sharing new levels of material prosperity. And then, finally, complete the mixture with a spirituality which puts far greater emphasis on ourselves, our feelings and discerning the specific plans God has for our lives. If we're not careful, this combination could become toxic.

Mention the term 'prosperity gospel' and most of us will immediately conjure up mental images of larger-than-life tele-evangelists making outrageous claims about the blessings which God will give to those who follow their teachings. Make a contribution to the new private jet or the refurbished broadcasting studio and wait for the good times to roll.

I'm sure that many of us would be appalled if it were suggested that we believe in a prosperity gospel. I'm not denying the importance of seeking God's wisdom and guidance for the crucial decisions each of us has to make in our lives, questions such as whom to marry and where to live and work. But I also believe we need to acknowledge the dangers which can come with this way of thinking and the need for all of us to be self-aware and honest with ourselves as we reflect on how God is at work in our lives.

When He spoke about the way God distributes His blessing, Jesus suggested an approach which seems to fly in the face of many of our assumptions. He describes His Father in heaven as one who 'causes his sun to rise on the evil and the good, and sends rain on the righteous and the unrighteous' (Matthew 5:45). Many of us might be troubled by the apparently arbitrary nature of God's blessing which is described here but we need to pay attention to the implication of Jesus' teaching. I'm sure there are occasions when the blessing which comes our way is the result of God's intervention in our lives, His direct answer to our prayers. But there will be other moments when the benefits we experience are part and parcel of the generous provision God is lavishing on lots of other people around, irrespective of whether they acknowledge Him as the gift-giver. We bought the same shares as everyone else in the stock flotation. We lived through the same property boom as our neighbours.

I am not denying that God wants us to seek His will for our lives and wants to provide for our needs. I believe this is true because of moments of inexplicable provision which I can't describe as anything other than God's intervention, times when money to pay the bills was posted through the door anonymously or when job opportunities came out of nowhere. But there have also been moments when my prayers didn't seem to be answered in the way I would have preferred and I've seen this pattern played out in the lives of people around me. I've known many fellow Christians who are faithful and earnest in seeking God's guidance and provision. Some are wealthy and some have struggled in poverty all their lives. Some have been healthy and others have longed for healing and kept on battling with illness, and why the blessing came to one and not the other remains to me a mystery. But then I remember how Jesus also told His followers that 'Foxes have dens and birds have nests, but the Son of Man has nowhere to lay his head' (Matthew 8:20). And this reminds me of another temptation which we constantly need to be battling against, the belief that God is showing up only in the good times and that following Him guarantees us a free pass from hardship.

Is there any language we can find which might allow us to express how God is relating to us, in a healthier way? It might be helpful to think about the difference between God *caring* for us and God *indulging* us, the difference between our belief in His love for us which extends to even the minor details of our lives ('You discern my going out and my lying down; you are familiar with all my ways' [Psalm 139:3]) and a theology which presumes He is ordering the world solely on our terms, a theology which allows us to give thanks for the blessings which come from His provision and intervention in our lives but which also recognises and laments the disorder and injustice in our world which affect our neighbours near and far away.

Attending to these issues is important because the beliefs we have about how God is working personally in our lives are always more than personal. They spill over into the attitudes we hold and the assumptions we make about what is happening in the lives of others. As recently as 2015, 96 per cent of Evangelical Alliance survey respondents affirmed their belief that 'Everyone has a duty to work to support themselves and their family if they can',[17] while 11 per cent agreed with the statement that 'if we are faithful we will prosper materially'.[18] In the same survey, evangelicals were asked what they considered to be the top causes of poverty in the UK. Only 33 per cent saw 'educational inequality' as an issue, and only 37 per cent believed 'inequality or social justice' to be a factor. However, 75 per cent of evangelicals considered 'laziness' to be a problem, and 84 per cent cited 'welfare dependency'.[19]

It's important to note that other surveys of evangelicals reveal an awareness of the dangers of materialism and excessive wealth. In a 2015 survey, examining the extent to which they identify with the values of the wider population described in the British Social Attitudes Survey, 1,730 evangelicals were asked to list what they regard as the most negative traits in British society. Sixty-five per cent of respondents cited consumerism, 58 per cent obsession with celebrity and 51 per cent sexual promiscuity.[20] Yet it's tempting to suggest that we express concern about a materialistic culture without realising our own collusion with it, even the extent to which the culture and politics of Britain, reshaped since the 1980s when constraints from capitalism were systematically removed, have been influenced by a particular strain of evangelical

Christianity. And that takes us to the story of one of the most influential British leaders of the twentieth century and how her values which reshaped the country were shaped by the faith of her youth.

'The New Testament is preoccupied with the individual': Mrs Thatcher and the evangelicals

Margaret Thatcher's upbringing could be considered as providing a textbook example of the values of Nonconformist Middle England. One of the great influences upon her life was her father, Alfred Roberts: owner of two grocery shops in Grantham, Lincolnshire, a member of the Rotary Club, part-time Justice of the Peace, president of the Board of Trade, school governor, local councillor and, last but not least, a faithful attender and regular preacher at Finkin Street Methodist Church. [21] It was this same church where Margaret attended services each Sunday, morning and evening services supplemented by Sunday school. Within this environment, she developed a view of the world predicated on a faith which was intensely personal and aligned to an emphasis on responsibility and hard work, a perspective that would eventually revolutionise Britain.

One of the clearest expressions of Margaret Thatcher's understanding of her faith, and its relationship to social change, can be found in a speech she delivered in the parish of St Lawrence Jewry, in the City of London, in 1981. She observed:

> the New Testament is preoccupied with the individual, with his need for forgiveness and for the

Divine strength, which comes to those who sincerely accept it. Of course, we can deduce from it the teachings of the Bible principles of public as well as private morality; but, in the last resort, all these principles refer back to the individual in his relationship with others.[22]

It could be said that this statement, more than any others, sums up the theology of Margaret Thatcher, with the ultimate priority which it attaches to the beliefs and actions of the individual. From this view of the world, an ideology was born which created an environment in which many flourished, exploiting the new opportunities which came from initiatives such as the sale of council homes, the privatisation of government-owned industries and new rules for the City and financial institutions. However, a heavy cost was borne by many who were caught up in the rapid changes of the 1980s, including those who lost their jobs (many working in traditional heavy industries) as rising unemployment was deemed a price worth paying to bring down inflation.

Mrs Thatcher's programme was one which generated plenty of opposition, not least from the church. But it's telling that the most vocal of these critics were prominent leaders of the Church of England. Their most famous assessment of the impact of government policy came in the 1985 report, *Faith in the City*, which expressed grave concerns about the effect of unemployment and poverty, especially in inner cities.

The report argued that the Church:

must question all economic philosophies, not least those which, when put into practice, have contributed to the blighting of whole districts, which do not offer the hope of amelioration, and which perpetuate the human misery and despair to which we have referred. The situation requires the Church to question from its own particular standpoint the morality of these economic philosophies.[23]

It seems more than a coincidence that the most vocal church criticism came from one which is shaped around a parish model which has, at its heart, a commitment to place, and which necessarily requires a presence in every community in the country, from urban to rural and everything in between. Such an emphasis on place differs markedly from the focus on the individual which we've discovered to be central to the evangelical and Nonconformist mindset.

But there's another aspect of Margaret Thatcher's perspective which needs to be considered, which highlights an inherent weakness in any theology which limits God's dealings with us and His world to only what happens at the individual level. Mrs Thatcher's mission wasn't just to set free individuals, but also to liberalise markets. During the 1980s, 'market forces' was a term that took on a new significance, one which hints at the way our lives aren't just affected by individual decisions but by bigger structures and influences. The New Testament uses other language to describe these forces: 'the rulers … the authorities … the powers of this dark world … the spiritual forces of evil in the heavenly realms' (Ephesians 6:12).

Ultimately, Mrs Thatcher's Christianity was one which failed to pay attention to these systems and structures. And to find out more about the pitfalls of such a view we need to leave British shores momentarily and consider some lessons from Chicago.

A story from Chicago

Chicago has recently been described as 'arguably the capital of black America',[24] the city which gave the United States the first black Congressman elected in the north, the broadcasting sensation that was *The Oprah Winfrey Show* and, most famously of all, the first African American president. But the city is also regarded as one of the most racially segregated in the country. African Americans moved north to Chicago in the Great Migration of the first half of the twentieth century, but were prevented from moving into white neighbourhoods by a series of restrictive measures which included bank practices which limited access to mortgages and policies which blocked the development of public housing in these areas. As whites began to move to the suburbs after the Second World War and restrictive covenants were removed by court orders, African Americans took up residence in many neighbourhoods in the city's south and west sides, a change which dramatically altered Chicago's demographics: 'In one generation, a third of the city's community areas went from monolithically white to monolithically black.'[25]

The disturbing story of how some of Chicago's churches responded to these changes has recently been told by the American academic Mark Mulder.[26] Mulder's work is a study of seven Christian Reformed Church communities, Dutch-heritage believers with a background of Calvinist theology and a congregational model of church. Each of these churches faced significant change in their neighbourhoods as African Americans moved into the Englewood and Roseland districts where they lived. We might imagine that their response could have been to welcome these newcomers and the new perspectives brought by their different experiences and theological perspectives. But instead they simply relocated, each congregation taking itself off to a nearby white suburb. How could this be? How could so many churches collude with and perpetuate racial division in their city?

The picture that emerges in Mulder's story is one of an understanding of faith which makes believers responsible for their personal piety but which fails to challenge their complicity with systems which keep people trapped in poverty or isolation. In this school of thought, a priority for Christians is the sustaining of a personal relationship with God, to the exclusion of wider social issues. Individual members of these churches insisted that their personal morality allowed no room for racist attitudes but collectively they colluded with migration patterns which sustained racial segregation in the city. It was hard to read this story without memories being evoked of my own childhood in Northern Ireland. In spite of the conflict in our society that brought death and injury on a weekly basis, each Sunday we attended church only to hear yet another reminder about the need for individual salvation.

I find it hard to recall sermons on themes such as peacemaking or reconciliation. Among the many tragic aspects of the thirty years of the 'Troubles' is the fact that they took place in an area where church attendance was far higher than the rest of the United Kingdom.[27] It is little wonder that some traditional churches in the Province, having offered so little to a divided society in its time of conflict, are seen as increasingly irrelevant in a time of peace.

Reflecting on Mulder's account of Chicago, I find myself wondering about my own complicity with the widening inequality in my own society. I ask myself about how much time I've invested in growing my personal faith, reading and studying, when I could have been getting to know my neighbours instead. None of us set out to do this deliberately, but the busyness of our church and personal routines can so easily overwhelm us and make it hard for us to see beyond our own pressing and immediate challenges.

As Mulder lists other reasons which explain evangelical departure from Englewood and Roseland, I am struck by the similarities between their experience and my own. For many believers, their primary relationships were with other members of a congregation rather than those who lived in their neighbourhood, another reflection of the way faith was lived in a dislocated bubble with no connection to a physical space.[28] It also appears that the privilege and wealth of some of these white evangelicals made it hard for them to really understand the challenges and prejudices faced by others living nearby. Well-intentioned we may be, but if we live in material comfort and without anxiety about how to pay the bills or pay for the shopping, we will probably find it impossible to truly appreciate the extent of the struggle to get by which is experienced by people living closer to us than we think.

In 2005, delivering the commencement address at Kenyon College, the American author David Foster Wallace told the following well-known story:

> There are these two young fish swimming along, and they happen to meet an older fish, swimming the other way. The older fish nods at them: 'Morning, boys, how's the water?' The two young fish swim on for a bit, and then one looks over at the other. 'What the hell is water?'[29]

The story offers an important reminder of the way in which aspects of our culture can become so much a part of the landscape of our lives that we barely notice the influence they are having upon us. We think of ourselves as 'in the world but not of it' (see John 17:14-16), often defining our position on issues such as sexual morality or the consumption of alcohol, oblivious to the ways in which the principalities and powers operate in economic models which we take for granted.

It's impossible to completely separate ourselves from the culture around us, and also important to bear in mind that Scripture doesn't tell us to do so anyway. As with so many issues, there's a tension to be held here. The early Christians were urged to come out of Babylon so as to escape God's coming judgement on the empire (Revelation 18:4). That command is found in Revelation, written to a church suffering persecution from the Roman

Empire but where Babylon is the symbol of all worldly powers which set themselves up against God's purposes. But 600 years earlier, when a group of Jewish exiles found themselves in the real Babylon, God reminded them of the importance of putting down roots and seeking the blessing of the place which was to be their home for the foreseeable future (Jeremiah 29:1-10).

This is the balancing act to which we're called, seeking the peace of our communities and cities while also making sure not to sell out to the values of the wider culture. We've already reflected on how the personal approach to faith which is prevalent in many of our churches is a reflection of our evangelical heritage, but it's time to consider one more influence upon us: the individualism which is the air we all breathe in twenty-first-century British culture.

If we cannot completely remove ourselves from the world, we can at least develop a greater awareness about the ways in which we are influenced by it. A first step on this journey might be a recognition of how the individualism of our evangelical faith reflects not just the heritage of our churches but also that of society.

All around us: the rise of individualism

One of the pitfalls of not being aware of the water we're swimming in can be our failure to realise that the currents are changing and that we're being swept along in the process. Among the most significant developments in Western society has been the increasingly fragmented and individualised nature of our lives, transitions which have gathered pace since the end of the Second World War.

Home life in Britain has seen immeasurable change in this period.[30] The increasing availability of television meant that families spent less of their leisure time at the pub or club and more in the homes which were being enthusiastically self-improved by their owner-occupiers. As with so many of these developments which began in the 1950s and 1960s, the pace of change has continued and even gathered pace since the turn of the century. The closure of large numbers of public houses in Britain in recent years can partly be explained by our increasing tendency to buy wine at the supermarket and drink it at home instead of enjoying beer at the pub.[31] Another reason for the fragmentation of community relationships has been the growing availability of personal transport. Motorists can commute in privacy, with the car also enabling them to shop, play (and worship) away from their own areas.

In more recent years, the intensity of some of these changes has increased further. At one time even television offered some occasions of national unity. I still have vivid memories of the dramatic decision taken in 1983 by *Coronation Street*'s Deirdre Barlow to turn her back on her lover, Mike Baldwin, returning to married life with Ken. While living every moment of the suspense herself, my mother also spoke excitedly of how many other people were speculating on how the story would unfold, with the outcome even displayed on the half-time scoreboard at Manchester United's Old Trafford ground: 'Ken 1 Mike 0'.

Rarely, today, does the whole nation come together in this way. The availability of a vast new selection of TV channels has been followed by the rise of the internet and the increasing use of portable devices which means that even *within* a home it's possible for different family members to be entertaining themselves alone. Instead of making us more knowledgeable and connected with one another, there is evidence that the internet is actually having the opposite effect. Overwhelmed by the sheer amount of information available online, many of us now retreat into smaller corners of the web, clicking only on links from sources or friends we trust. Instead of broadening our horizons, the internet becomes an echo chamber for most users, a place where our existing views of the world are reinforced. We listen to music, watch films and eat at restaurants recommended by communities of like-minded people,[32] oblivious to the algorithms of social-media companies who keep us in our own little bubbles, ensuring that the stories we see and the links we can click on reflect our own particular interests.

We also need to recognise the impact of our long working-hours culture. The average British working week now totals 43.6 hours, compared to a European figure of 40.3,[33] with both parents now working full-time in 45.5 per cent of couple households.[34] When so much time is spent in the workplace, it is hardly surprising that what little leisure time is left is jealously guarded by hard-pressed families. These increasing pressures are often cited to explain a lack of civic engagement in Western societies.

Not everyone agrees with this analysis. Although levels of voter turnout are falling, along with the membership of traditional organisations such as trade unions, the Women's Institute and churches, it's been noted that some pressure groups and charities are seeing an increase in support.[35] But to become a member or supporter of the Woodland Trust or Oxfam, for example, may require nothing more than filling out a Direct Debit instruction form or agreeing to receive the emails which fill the inboxes of many so-called 'slacktivists'. It's not that we fail to care about issues relating to the environment or social justice, but the busyness of our own routines means it's often easier to hit the retweet button or share a link than it is to share our time or open our homes to others.

It could be argued that individualism is the natural human reaction to the relentless pace of life and change in our society, a survival instinct of those under pressure: the only way we can survive a long day at the office or on the road is to hibernate each evening with a bottle of wine and Netflix. However, other research indicates that this doesn't need to be the case: a 2010 UK charities report suggested that 'individuals and cultures that attach greater importance to self-transcendence and openness-to-change values' are more likely to show 'greater concern about bigger-than-self problems, and higher motivation to address these problems'. The same report suggests that in a similar way, individuals and societies who attach high value to self-enhancement are found to be 'less concerned about global conflict and the abuse of human rights, more prejudiced towards outsiders'.[36] Deciding that charity begins at home is not an inevitable human response in times of crisis; people can be conditioned to act towards others in a spirit of generosity and vulnerability. It's tempting to consider how much of this 'openness-to-change' is encouraged in many of our churches, especially in those where the emphasis has been on stressing our difference and separation from others or even a suspicious resentment towards the inclusiveness of wider society.

Another counterpoint to the suggestion that we've become a culture of individuals turned in on ourselves is offered by those who point to the emergence of the many different groups which offer opportunities to participate in various types of self-help or self-improvement. Think, for example, of Weight Watchers, a keep-fit or mindfulness class, or even the many book clubs which have become so popular in recent years. Such groups have undoubtedly been the means of deepening relationships and broadening horizons for many people, but it's hard to escape the sense that their focus is less on community service and more on how we can grow as individuals.

Could it be argued that a similar shift has taken place in our churches, where regular home group discussions have now become the focal point of congregational life for many Christians in recent decades? There are many benefits from these groups, which provide opportunities for deeper fellowship, accountability and discussion about how faith is lived out in everyday situations. But could it be that their popularity is evidence of ways we've been influenced by our wider culture, that the focus of our discipleship has shifted from public witness to private opinions and inward-looking relationships?

I am not suggesting that we cast aside our theology of conversion, but I do think it's time for a fresh conversation about what we are converting people from, and what we are discipling them into. The vision of the church which we discover in the New Testament is not one of assorted individuals, each separately discovering that a relationship with Jesus might be the means by which they can become the best possible version of themselves. Instead, the early Christians discovered that they were becoming part of a story far bigger than any one person. They knew that the new work God had done in Jesus had ushered in a 'new humanity', not only restoring His relationship with people but removing the barriers which cause division between them (Ephesians 2:14-22), and they understood their mission in putting the values of this new kingdom on display. Wives and husbands, children and parents, slaves and masters, all were to relate to each other in new ways 'in Christ', demonstrating the difference between their outlook and the attitudes of a world which ordered by power and hierarchy (Ephesians 5:21 – 6:9). These new attitudes weren't just lived out within the confines of the church, they overflowed into love for enemies and a concern for the needs of the poor and marginalised. Even in the times when the new movement struggled to come to terms with the challenges of preaching to and welcoming both Jews and Gentiles, its leaders were able to find common ground in their agreement on the need to 'remember the poor' (Galatians 2:10).

In recent years, many churches have rediscovered the importance of this service of the disadvantaged. Our buildings are often open seven days a week, providing food and advice on debt, job clubs and night shelters. But could it be that we are living in kingdom ways, without thinking in kingdom ways, creating an unnecessary tension for many who are struggling to understand the significance of their actions? We give someone food, but with a nagging sense of regret if our interaction with them doesn't create the opportunity to speak of Jesus? We open the church on a weekday to offer friendship and support to lonely parents and toddlers, but with a sadness that few if any will join our worship on Sunday? We suggest ways in which someone can find a way out of debt, but with a sense of quiet contentment about the ways in which our hard work and faithfulness have prevented us from falling into such hardship. We seek to serve those on the margins of our community without ever shaking off our conviction that the real business of the church is done on Sunday, in the space of worship songs and Bible-reading and preaching which will deepen our devotion to God and inform our knowledge of Him. It can feel as if we're living in two worlds in the space of life in one congregation, barely understanding the strain we place on ourselves by our failure to appreciate the distance between them. Isn't there a better, healthier way of approaching these issues?

Time for a bigger story

A recently launched campaign by evangelical leaders aims to address what is perceived as a problem of decreased 'confidence in the Gospel'.[37] A picture is painted of churches socially engaged, but experiencing 'an apparent decrease in our confidence and competence to verbally explain the good news'. But perhaps that lack of assurance is not about the gospel per se but rather a narrow and privatised version of it which appears not to be fit for purpose when it confronts the harsh reality of life for the people we aim to serve. When we're faced with someone who comes to a foodbank because they haven't eaten in a week, it seems crass to tell them that their most pressing question is what would happen to their soul if they faced imminent death. When we're speaking with someone about how they can cope with the insurmountable debt they're in and the payments demanded by creditors, it doesn't seem the right time to mention that God loved the world so much that He sent Jesus.

But what if the message we had to share was of a story bigger than just individual salvation? What if the hope we proclaimed extended beyond an eternal reward enjoyed in a time and place so far removed from our present reality?

What if the appeal we made went something like this? We all know that something is wrong with our world. Every day we witness the reality of sin and evil. We experience it in our own lives, in sickness, in the failure of relationships, in our own inability to break habits which are destructive for us and the people we share life with. And we see it when we turn on the news and learn of the latest story of suffering caused by injustice or natural disaster. But one day everything will be better, God is going to bring in a new future when all shall be made right. 'Death will be no more; mourning and crying and pain will be no more, for the first things have passed away' (Revelation 21:4, NRSV). And this future can be experienced right now, a glimpse of it can be seen in the church, the community of those who have trusted in Jesus and are putting on display a kingdom which welcomes male and female, slave and free, Jew and Gentile (Galatians 3:28).

The kingdom has not fully arrived, and the task of bringing it belongs not to us but to God. However, we can order our lives in ways which look ahead to God's complete redemption and renewal, ways which mean that crossing the threshold of our churches is also entering a glimpse and foretaste of something reconciled and at peace, the way everything will look one day.

A story which puts flesh on the bones of these ideas can be found in Luke 19's report of Jesus' encounter with Zacchaeus. Luke locates this incident near the end of his 'travel narrative', his account of the journey Jesus makes with His disciples from Galilee to Jerusalem. Zacchaeus comes across as a figure who embodies many of the themes which Luke explores in his Gospel. He is rich, having made lots of money from his collusion with the Roman occupiers, but he is also an outsider, someone ostracised by his own people. In that respect, he is little different from the widow, tax collector, children and blind beggar of whom Luke has written in the previous chapter.[38] Like the paralysed man in Luke 5, Zacchaeus is unable to get close to Jesus: 'He wanted to see who Jesus was, but because he was short he could not see over the crowd' (Luke 19:3).

When he finally comes face to face with Jesus, Zacchaeus responds to Him in a manner which is strikingly different from the rich ruler of Luke 18. Having been told by Jesus to 'Sell everything you have and give to the poor' (Luke 18:22), this privileged figure finds he cannot bring himself to make the sacrifices demanded from him. On the other hand, the outsider Zacchaeus promises to give half of his possessions to the poor, while also offering compensation of four times the amount he has taken fraudulently from his victims.

This remarkable story, one where poor victims are blessed by repentance and compensation from the privileged and where a rich man discovers freedom from the corrupt and exploitative practices in which he is caught up, finishes with one of the most famous statements of Jesus in Luke's Gospel: 'Today salvation has come to this house ... For the Son of Man came to seek and to save the lost' (Luke 19:9-10).

The language used here is telling. 'Salvation' is one of Luke's favourite words in his account of Jesus' life and ministry. Time and again it is used in his Gospel to describe the difference made to those whose lives are changed by an encounter with Jesus: the healing of a man's withered hand, the release of a man possessed by demons and the cleansing of a leper are just a few examples.[39] Now we find the same terminology applied to this account of a move from greed to generosity, which also turns out to be a means of blessing and freedom for those who have been the victims of the tax collector's exploitative practices.

Such liberation cannot come without a cost. In recent years, lots of our churches have been preoccupied with issues of human sexuality. These conversations have often been painful, but there is at least an increased willingness on the part of many to acknowledge the pain caused by old attitudes and the need for more honest dialogue. But can the same thing be said about our approach to money? How can we discuss this issue in congregations where those with savings worship alongside those in debt, where recently retired and affluent baby boomers stand shoulder to shoulder with a younger generation working longer hours and facing the prospect of living as 'generation rent' for the foreseeable future?

Given that what we earn and we do with it might now be more of a taboo than what goes on in the bedroom, these conversations would need to be approached sensitively, shoes taken off as we tread on each other's holy ground. But, handled with care, they might be the means of creating a liberating honesty in our churches, a recognition that what enslaves us and dehumanises us often has as much to do with economics as it does with sexual morality, that our individualistic culture needs to be challenged in the name of Jesus who spoke of love for God and neighbour as the greatest commandment (Matthew 22:34-40).

Could it be that all this time we've been searching for connection and fulfilment in all the wrong places, a reflection of the ways we can so easily compartmentalise our lives? We think of worship on Sunday and the midweek discussion group as the places we go to in order to learn and deepen relationships, the places to 'receive', and then we 'give' in our social projects, often relating to people in more guarded ways which reflect the different expectations we have of our encounters with those whose immediate needs are being met.

But what if we entered into each activity of our day open to an encounter with God and other people, irrespective of the roles we are playing or the task in hand? Might we discover that connection is often a thing which happens naturally, when we're least looking for it, and that a sense of personal contentment is among 'these things … given to you as well' (Matthew 6:33) when we make the kingdom our number one priority?

Samuel Smiles is no longer the celebrity figure which he was to our Victorian forebears. But his ideas, and those of his Victorian evangelical contemporaries, still cast their shadow over many of our churches, where the actions of the kingdom and a privatised view of faith all too often collide with each other. The moment has come when our thinking and talking needs to catch up with our doing.

Until this happens, we will continue to experience the stress and strain which comes from living in two worlds. It's time to bridge the gap.

For discussion

1. How do you react to the suggestion that some of us might have a set of beliefs which come closer to the term 'prosperity gospel' than we might care to admit?
2. Can you think of ways in which our modern lives seem to be becoming more individualistic, in addition to the ones listed above? Are there practical steps which local churches could take to resist these changes?
3. Do you agree with issues raised in this chapter concerning church small groups? How can we ensure that such groups look outwards as well as inwards?
4. What do you think of the suggestion that when we proclaim the gospel we need to tell 'a bigger story', one which speaks about the kingdom as much as about individual salvation? Would this story be more or less attractive to the people you know?
5. Is it really realistic to think that we could talk with honesty about money and our financial decisions in church? What would be the impact if we did?

Notes

[1] An introduction to the life and work of Samuel Smiles can be found in Asa Briggs, *Victorian People* (London: Penguin,1955),

pp 124-147. A more recent reflection on his cultural significance is available from Dominic Sandbrook, *The Great British Dream Factory* (London: Allen Lane, 2015), pp 407-435.

[2] Briggs, *Victorian People*, p 129.

[3] Sandbrook, *The Great British Dream Factory*, p 431.

[4] Ibid, p 431.

[5] See Mike Savage, *Social Class in the 21st Century* (London: Pelican, 2015), p 30.

[6] D W Bebbington, *Evangelicalism in Modern Britain: A History from the 1730s to 1980s* (London: Routledge, 1989), p 2.

[7] See Michael Horton, *Ordinary: Sustainable Faith in a Radical, Restless World* (Grand Rapids, MI: Zondervan, 2014), p 73.

[8] William Abraham, *The Logic of Evangelism* (Grand Rapids, MI: Eerdmans, 1989), p 58.

[9] http://www.alliancenet.org/mos-beta/1517/the-continuing-influence-of-charles-finney (accessed 11th July 2019).

[10] http://eauk.org/connect/about-us/history.cfm (accessed 5th July 2019).

[11] See B G Worrall, *The Making of the Modern Church: Christianity in England since 1800* (revised edition) (London: SPCK, 1993), p 137.

[12] http://www.qmulreligionandliterature.co.uk/research/the-dissenting-academies-project/legislation/ (accessed 5th July 2019).

[13] D W Bebbington, 'Spurgeon and the Common Man', *Baptist Review of Theology*, Vol 5 No 1, 1995, p 71.

[14] Bebbington, 'Spurgeon and the Common Man', p 69.

[15] Michael Goodman, 'Numerical Decline amongst English Baptists 1930-1939', *Baptist Quarterly*, Vol XXXVI, 1996, p 298.

[16] See Roy Hattersley, *The Catholics* (London: Chatto & Windus, 2017), pp 422-423.

[17] Evangelical Alliance, 'Good News for the Poor? A Snapshot of the Beliefs and Habits of Evangelical Christians in the UK – Summer 2015', p 7.

[18] EA, 'Good News for the Poor?', p 7.

[19] EA, 'Good News for the Poor?', p 14.

[20] For more details, see http://www.eauk.org/idea/british-values.cfm (accessed 5th July 2019).

[21] For a detailed discussion of the influences of nonconformism upon Margaret Thatcher, see Eliza Filby, *God and Mrs Thatcher: The Battle for Britain's Soul* (London: Biteback Publishing, 2015), pp 1-44.

[22] https://www.margaretthatcher.org/document/104587 (accessed 11th July 2019).

[23] *Faith in the City: A Call for Action by Church and Nation: The Report of the Archbishop of Canterbury's Commission on Urban Priority Areas* (London: Church House Publishing,1985), p 208.

[24] https://www.theguardian.com/commentisfree/2017/jan/08/racial-segregation-chicago-ills-america-too (accessed 5th July 2019).

[25] http://www.nbcchicago.com/blogs/ward-room/White-Flight-By-The-Numbers-206302551.html (accessed 5th July 2019).

[26] See Mark Mulder, *Shades of White Flight: Evangelical Congregations and Urban Departure* (New Brunswick, NJ: Rutgers University Press, 2015).

[27] https://cain.ulster.ac.uk/ni/religion.htm#3 (accessed 13th June 2019).

[28] See Mulder, Shades of White Flight, p 78.

[29] http://bulletin-archive.kenyon.edu/x4280.html (accessed 11th July 2019).

[30] For a more detailed overview of these changes, see Ian Jones, *The Local Church and Generational Change in Birmingham 1945-2000* (Woodbridge: Boydell Press, 2012), p 141ff.

[31] See Christopher Snowdon, *Closing Time: Who's Killing the British Pub?* (London: Institute of Economic Affairs, 2014), p 13.
[32] See Margaret Heffernan, *Wilful Blindness: Why We Ignore the Obvious at Our Peril* (London: Simon & Schuster, 2011), p 24.
[33] http://www.ibtimes.co.uk/burnout-britain-long-work-hours-culture-returns-warns-tuc-1519158 (accessed 5th July 2019).
[34] https://www.ons.gov.uk/employmentandlabourmarket/peopleinwork/employmentandemployeetypes/articles/familiesandthelabourmarketengland/2018 (accessed 10th July 2019).
[35] See Matthew Hilton, James McKay, Nicholas Crowson and Jean-François Mouhot, *The Politics of Expertise: How NGOs Shaped Modern Britain* (Oxford: Oxford University Press, 2013), pp 1-2.
[36] Tom Crompton, *Common Cause: The Case for Working with Our Cultural Values* (Godalming: WWF, 2010), p 32.
[37] http://www.eauk.org/church/campaigns/confidence-in-the-gospel/about.cfm (accessed 5th July 2019).
[38] See Joel Green, The New International Commentary on the New Testament: The Gospel of Luke (Grand Rapids: Eerdmans, 1997), p 666.
[39] In Luke 6:9 and 17:19, it is Jesus Himself speaking; in Luke 8:36, the word *sōzō* is used by Luke himself. Other uses of the word can be found in Luke 7:50; 8:12; 8:48; 9:24; 17:19; 18:42. For an overview of 'The Call to Salvation' as one of the theological themes of Luke, see Robert H Stein, *The New American Commentary: Luke* (Nashville, TN: Broadman & Holman, 1992), pp 50-51.

Chapter Two
The Gap between Expectations and Experience

Many years ago, I heard a joke about two cows standing in a field. One day, a lorry from a dairy went past with words emblazoned along its side proclaiming the properties of what was for sale: 'Fresh milk: pasteurised, homogenised, organic, semi-skimmed.' One cow turns to the other and says, 'Darling, one feels so inadequate these days.'[1]

Most of us will know how she feels. For the sake of my sanity, I've learned that it's best not to pay too much attention to advertising, which often seems only to serve the purpose of laying bare my many inadequacies, one reminder layered upon another about the levels of wealth, style and fitness that I ought to have attained by now. I need to be driving that SUV, ideally with my good-looking family to a day at the beach which begins with surfing and ends with a barbecue. I need a smartphone and a smartwatch, and various other products whose existence I am not yet aware of, perhaps a smart toaster (this would be controlled by an app, meaning that I could instruct it to produce perfectly golden toast to await me on my return from my daily five-mile run). I need to be fit. I need to be good at DIY. Ideally, I would also have a voluminous and perfectly manicured hipster beard.

But it often feels as if the weight of expectations isn't just restricted to the things we wear or the objects we acquire. Sadly, the same sense of not living up to what others want from us is often felt in our churches too. If anyone insists that 'size doesn't matter', tell them to eavesdrop on a conversation between two church leaders. Sooner or later the question will be posed: 'How many do you get on a Sunday morning?' And the pressures don't end there. As I survey the websites of other churches and look at the promotional material they produce, I find myself confronted with numerous reminders of what I have not yet become. I need a bigger worship band and a more attractive building. I need to be running that innovative new outreach programme, alongside my men's group, women's group and other activities for people of all ages. And then I read the profiles of the church leaders, trying not to feel too inadequate when I come across another voluminous and perfectly manicured hipster beard.

As we all know, there is nothing which robs us of our joy and contentment faster than comparison. We can all find someone who is richer, thinner, more gifted or successful than we are, and if they're not currently known to us a quick search on the internet will soon alert us to their presence. Tools such as Twitter and Facebook provide the perfect platform for self-promotion, with many church leaders projecting, like the rest of us, not every detail of their lives but an edited version for public consumption which accentuates the successes and omits references to the frustrations. We trawl through the feeds and the timelines and quickly we find the doubts surfacing in our minds. Why haven't we thought of that? Why wasn't I invited to that meeting?

Sometimes, the comparisons which disconcert us the most aren't even with contemporary people or situations. Many of us feel the weight of the past bearing down on us, the stories of the days when the Sunday school numbered 100 children and the Boys' Brigade had a waiting list. Even the size of our buildings can become a source of insecurity, smaller congregations gathering to meet in large spaces, sometimes literally overshadowed by an empty gallery, and wondering what it was like when each pew was filled with worshippers (if ever such a time existed).

What does success look like? And what is that to you?

Before training to become a church leader I spent almost ten years of life working in industry, and was involved in the delivery of countless projects. At the planning stage of each one there was a question we would invariably ask: What does success look like?

It didn't feel like it at the time, but I now look back on those project meetings with a sense of wistfulness about the lack of complications we faced when deciding how effective we had been. Success was defined as a set of changes delivered on time and within budget, or improved customer satisfaction statistics. It's harder, however, to quantify achievements in the life of the church. What units of measurement do we use? The rise of Sunday morning attendance, the growth of the ministry team? Or how about the development of virtues or the fruit of the Spirit?

How can we compare the ministry of a smaller church struggling to sustain its witness and service to its community on limited numbers and budgets with that of the larger, better-resourced congregation just down the road? How do we account for the effectiveness of church leaders whose hours might be spread across multiple smaller congregations or those who lead in contexts where buildings are in decay and worshippers beset by anxiety? Taking into account the biblical picture of how 'One sows and another reaps' (John 4:37), how can we accurately measure the ministry of the many churches who incubate the faith of young people who never return home after university studies? Talk to many church leaders and I'll wager that at least some of them will ruefully refer to a drain of talent away from poorer communities and churches to those which are already well-resourced: 'to those who have, more will be given' (Matthew 13:12, NRSV).

For some churches, simply sustaining a presence in an area where many people are worn down by hardship or hopelessness may require enormous tenacity and faithfulness. In other situations, brave and courageous leadership will be required to imagine how witness may need to be expressed differently as an area faces demographic or economic change. Nor can we escape the fact that these issues are being faced against a backdrop of declining church attendance, with all the associated pressures this places on budgets and the lingering suspicion that what is truly valued is something which can be immediately measured and quantified. Numbers trump virtues every time.

Near the end of John's Gospel, we find Jesus Himself warning the disciples of the danger of comparison. Having just been restored following his denial of Jesus:

> Peter turned and saw that the disciple whom Jesus loved was following them. (This was the one who had leaned back against Jesus at the supper and had said, 'Lord, who is going to betray you?') When Peter saw him, he asked, 'Lord, what about him?' Jesus answered, 'If I want him to remain alive until I return, what is that to you? You must follow me.'
> *John 21:20-22*

Any one of us with even a shred of self-awareness will recognise something of ourselves in Peter at this moment. In spite of being fresh from the most intimate of encounters with Jesus, a sin forgiven about which deep guilt will have been felt and a relationship healed after wondering if reconciliation might ever be possible, Peter cannot resist the temptation to look over his shoulder. What will happen to John, he wonders: will he achieve a position of more prominent leadership? Has there always been something bigger and better planned for 'the disciple whom Jesus loved'? Will John travel further or build something bigger for the kingdom? Jesus' answer, to the question voiced by Peter and all the other ones swirling round his head, is telling: 'If I want him to remain alive until I return, what is that to you? You must follow me.'

Peter is told simply to focus on living out the particular call which God will place upon his life, to resist the distraction of preoccupation with what others are building.

Looking over our shoulders: Church and the *Hello!* culture

Few may have realised it at the time, but 2nd September 1944 was a seminal date in Western popular culture. A young newspaper journalist, Antonio Sánchez Gómez, had dreamt of launching a 'weekly illustrated journal devoted to "the froth of life", showing readers the lives of the rich and famous as light relief from the ravages of war'.[2] Unfortunately, the first edition of *¡Hola!* magazine, with an artist's illustration on the front cover, failed to make an impression on readers. In response to disappointing sales figures, Gómez then had the bright idea of placing a photo of Clark Gable on the cover of the second week's edition which duly flew off the news stands.

So began a publishing sensation, which arrived in Britain in 1988, joined two years later by *OK!*, a rival which shamelessly mimicked the format of the original. Many of us will be familiar with the formula of the magazines, a heady blend of celebrity gossip and fashion advice: pictures of the stunning dress worn by a beautiful actress at the latest Hollywood film premiere, alongside details of the £40 replica available on the high street; reports on who attended and what was worn at the latest A-listed wedding; beautiful celebrities announce their pregnancies alongside photos of their perfectly proportioned baby bumps, in anticipation of future articles which will include pictures of aforementioned offspring and details of how Mum miraculously regained her pre-pregnancy figure. At best, the magazines are a celebration of materialism and vanity, and at their worst promote a slightly sinister form of voyeurism. Most famous of all are the 'home visit interviews' published by the magazines, where those in the limelight open the doors of their mansions, giving readers the opportunity to marvel at the luxury in which they live, to illustrate the interviews containing bland reflections on the latest events in their lives.

Of course, *Hello!* and *OK!* are not the only publications to specialise in celebrity journalism. But they are the perfect examples of our obsession with every detail of the lives of the rich and famous, from soap opera actors to singers to Premiership footballers. We look at the décor of their homes, we marvel at their perfect bodies clothed in the latest fashion and we wonder what it might take for us to have a little bit of what they have, and all the while we are robbed of our sense of what is real and realistic and our appreciation of what we already have. Like the psalmist, we find our feet slipping as we read enviously about the lives of those who:

> have no struggles;
> their bodies are healthy and strong.
> They are free from common human burdens;
> they are not plagued by human ills.
> *Psalm 73:4-5*

Only later does the writer realise the danger of such thinking – recognising how to carry on in this way would have resulted in a betrayal of others in the family of God's people – and recover a healthy perspective while worshipping with the faithful (Psalm 73:15-17).

But is there a danger that we run a similar risk of raising false expectations and comparing ourselves unhelpfully in the world of church? I've known for myself the blessings to be had from worship in a crowd of hundreds, or even thousands. I've been inspired and enlightened by the preaching I've heard at the same events. But then the festival ends and we find ourselves back at church the following Sunday and facing the same frustrations and eccentric personalities which were there when we left. The process of reacclimatising can be painful.

Of course, we are not the first generation to experience the phenomenon of the celebrity preacher or worship leader. In the nineteenth century, crowds numbering in the thousands flocked to theatres to hear the songs of Ira Sankey or the sermons of D L Moody. But this trend has undoubtedly been exacerbated by the new technology which brings us closer than ever to our spiritual heroes. Why listen to your pastor when you can download the latest thoughts of Boyd, Bell or Piper? Why sing those boring old Kendrick songs which are so 1990s at your local church when you can download the latest offering from Hillsong? The effect of this can often be to diminish the value of what we have locally, in light of the supposedly superior offer which is available online.[3]

Not everyone will agree with this criticism. Some will counter with the observation that we are blessed to have access to such a wealth of learning from gifted communicators. My concern is not with the quality of what is on offer, but rather its remoteness. I recognise that I cannot offer the congregation which I serve sermons which match the quality of those delivered by respected church leaders who top the charts on iTunes. But I can offer my presence, my willingness to enter into covenant relationship with them. I preach as one who lives in the community, who visits homes and hospitals, entering into the joy of marriages and baptisms and experiencing the pain of sickness and death. Sunday by Sunday, I stand before the congregation as one who knows them and is known by them, with my strengths and all my weaknesses, but loved nevertheless. I know when I enter our pulpit that I am not the best preacher 'out there', but I can validly claim to be the best preacher for this place because I have heard a call from these people, moved to be among them and entered into covenant with them. Surely, this is the only appropriate approach for those who proclaim that our good news is the story of one who 'became flesh and lived among us' (John 1:14, NRSV). Ours is a story of a God who seeks relationship with people, so much so that He comes as one of us, to live, work, eat, laugh, cry as each human does. To truly live out such a story requires a community; relationships with other men, women and children; people I can touch; food and wine I can taste; homes I can visit.

A similar appraisal could be offered of the various tools and techniques which many churches turn to, hoping they will turn out to be the silver-bullet answer to the questions they've asked about evangelism or declining numbers. It wasn't so long ago that many UK congregations traded in their home-grown vision statements and programmes for those famously espoused by Rick Warren in his best-seller, *The Purpose Driven Church*.[4] I don't deny that many of them will have gained a vision statement that was pithy and memorable and backed up by evidence of having delivered results consistently, but I wonder what was lost in the process, how many ended up like the corner shop taken over by Tesco, or the coffee bar which sold out to Starbucks, made to believe that church could be done 'off-the-shelf', forgetting the value of what is local and home-grown.

It would be wrong to give the impression that I have no respect for the principles outlined in *The Purpose Driven Church*. But my concern is that this model and others like it reduce the task of leadership to technique; following the instruction manual replaces the labour of love that is the task of listening to God, a church and a neighbourhood and discerning what expression of church might be most appropriate for a given context. Another problem of such technocratic methods is that they overlook the complexity of churches. The body of Christ is an organism and not a machine. Each local church is a beautiful but intricate creation, made up of people, each with gifts and talents as well as hurts and vested interests, and often influenced by the complications of their history and the spiritual powers operating in the congregation and the area. Churches need to be led, not operated by someone reading a manual, as if they could pull a lever at one point in a process and see the output, perfectly formed disciples, emerge at the other end.

Finally, I suspect that many churches who attempt to follow such approaches end up discovering that their neighbourhood isn't like Saddleback, California, nor is their pastor as talented as Rick Warren. We often learn that celebrated strategies for church growth cannot be replicated in different cultural contexts and without the energy and talents of the gifted leaders who have developed them.

A story which sheds light on these issues can be found in 1 Samuel 17, where the emerging figure of David steps forward to offer his services to Israel as the one willing to accept the challenge made by Goliath. Before he goes off to fight the Philistine champion, David receives some last-minute instructions from King Saul, who also dresses the young man in his armour. It's reported that: 'David fastened on his sword over the tunic and tried walking around, because he was not used to them' (1 Samuel 17:39). At this crucial moment in the story, David demonstrates a remarkable awareness of both his own strengths and weaknesses as well as the tactics required for this moment. He knew there was nothing to be gained from taking on the armour and approach of the existing king, an imitation act which would mean being untrue to who he really was.

David realised the dangers of taking on a giant in close combat, a manoeuvre which would have made it all too easy for Goliath, with his superior reach, to pick him off with his sword. And he also had confidence in his strengths. He didn't feel inadequate about his limitations with a sword because he knew how to use a sling, an apparently low-tech weapon which his enemy sneered at but one which turned out to be just what was needed to strike at him from a distance. Another risk of comparing ourselves with others is that we are so preoccupied with what we don't have that we fail to realise the means God has placed at our disposal, His particular equipping for the time and place in which we find ourselves.

An added insight into this story can be found in the book of Judges. In a description of the military capacity of the tribe of the Benjaminites, we read: 'Among all these soldiers there were seven hundred select troops who were left-handed, each of whom could sling a stone at a hair and not miss' (Judges 20:16). Many of us familiar with the story of David might consider the skills he used to defeat Goliath as verging on the miraculous, but this detail in Judges confirms that many others possessed the same ability to use a sling. Perhaps David's real strength lay in his capacity to see the potential in the skills he possessed and his willingness to take a risk in using them for God.[5]

'Nostalgia ain't what it used to be':[6] comparisons with the past

Often, we don't just feel we're falling short of the contemporary churches in our vicinity; we also sense a burden of history and our failure to sustain the size and models of church which thrived in previous generations, the days when Brigade groups were full or evening services attended by a significant number of people.

Could it also be the case that what we miss, even more than the attendance numbers or programmes of the past, is the sense of certainty and clarity which came from living in what seemed like a less complicated time? We long, deep down, for the return of a time when the church seemed to have more influence in and respect from wider society, when it could dictate terms on matters such as the definition of marriage, and when teaching was more black and white, when positions were clearly defined and locked down on issues such as sexuality, eternal punishment and models of the atonement.

In recent years, a number of writers have made extensive use of the language of exile to describe the church's experience of the loss of privilege and power[7] in what is often referred to as post-Christendom, a society where our laws and traditions continue to reflect our Christian heritage but against a backdrop of declining church attendance and increasing secularism. As we reflect on how to come to terms with the territory we're in, it's helpful to consider the different responses offered to the Jewish people by prophets who ministered at the time of the first exile, the moment at the beginning of the sixth century BC when Jerusalem was invaded, the temple ransacked and the brightest and best of Judah's young people taken to captivity in Babylon.

Two prophets who speak into this situation are Hananiah and Jeremiah, whose story is told in Jeremiah 28. In the previous chapter, Jeremiah's actions have marked him out as the stereotypical prophet of doom. As the armies of Babylon grow in strength, Jeremiah is commanded by God to 'Make a yoke out of straps and crossbars and put it on your neck' (Jeremiah 27:2). This yoke, the sort that would normally be worn by an ox pulling along agricultural equipment, is a symbol of the oppression which several countries are about to suffer at the hands of the Babylonian Empire, including the seventy years of exile for the Jewish people that he has previously prophesied (Jeremiah 25:12).

In chapter 28, however, an alternative future is spoken of by another prophet. Hananiah does not predict suffering or loss on the scale warned of by Jeremiah. Instead, he encourages the Jewish people to sit tight and wait for a time, within just two years, when the Babylonian threat will recede and artefacts taken from the temple by Nebuchadnezzar will be returned. To add to the drama of this prophetic face-off, Hananiah even goes so far as to forcibly remove the yoke worn by Jeremiah to symbolise the longer period of suffering he warned of.

It's been pointed out that at first glance Hananiah comes across as the more impressive, even plausible, figure in this story.[8] He has the physical strength to put Jeremiah in his place, he has a message which apparently offers more hope (two years of struggle versus seventy) and there is also historical precedent for his message. Just over a hundred years ago Jerusalem had faced a similar existential threat, the risk of invasion by Assyria. On that occasion God had promised deliverance for the city through the words of another prophet, Isaiah, words that came true. Why not believe that He can do it all again?

But as we read further through this book, we discover it's Jeremiah who's on the right side of the story. We are given no reason to doubt the sincerity of Hananiah's faith in God, and yet he comes across as a figure who is ultimately unable to grasp how Judah's situation has now changed and who fails to see that God's purposes are not to preserve Jerusalem but rather to make its people face the consequences of their sin. Babylon may well be the enemy of God's people, but He is now planning to use it to bring about His purposes.

The advice Jeremiah offers to the people is a tougher pill to swallow. Contrary to the notion that normal service will be resumed within two years, Jeremiah famously urges the exiles to face up to the reality of life in Babylon and get ready for the long haul:

> Build houses and settle down; plant gardens and eat what they produce. Marry and have sons and daughters; find wives for your sons and give your daughters in marriage, so that they too may have sons and daughters. Increase in number there; do not decrease. Also, seek the peace and prosperity of the city to which I have carried you into exile. Pray to the LORD for it, because if it prospers, you too will prosper.
> *Jeremiah 29:5-7*

These words are challenging on several levels. The exiles are not permitted to live out of suitcases. Instead they are to unpack their belongings and put all their effort into making new lives in Babylon. Building homes, planting gardens and establishing new long-term relationships are all ways in which they can demonstrate their commitment to their new location. Most startling of all is the command to 'seek the peace and prosperity' of Babylon. It's hard to imagine the impact of these words on the first recipients of this 'Letter to the Exiles', those who are pining for Jerusalem, the 'city of shalom', but who are now told to seek the peace of Babylon instead. It's not enough to dig in and only look after themselves in their new location, these exiles need to take responsibility for those around them.

What can this story teach churches who are coming to terms with dwindling resources and waning influence? There are hard questions raised here about who to listen to in moments of crisis. Hananiah appears to offer hope but his answer to Jerusalem's dilemma seems too easy. We may be reassured by similar voices in our own time, who assure us that if we keep on doing what we've always done, God will one day restore all that has been lost. Ultimately, however, we may be better served by listening to those who are urging us to face the reality of our current situation and imagine how God might work within it, while also remembering that exile was not just a time of loss and despair. This was also a moment when poets and prophets imagined the possibility of return to Jerusalem and a new work of God: the valley of dry bones which come to life spoken of by Ezekiel (Ezekiel 37:1-14), Isaiah's vision of 'streams in the wasteland' (see Isaiah 43:14-21), and Jeremiah's promise of a new covenant (Jeremiah 31:31-34).

Have you ever attended a concert and found a familiar pattern being played out? The musician appears on stage ready to play material from their new album but the audience is only interested in hearing the greatest hits performed one more time. I sometimes wonder if this is a picture which describes many of our churches. We are clinging on tenaciously to what has worked in the past and denying God the opportunity for Him to bless us with the new thing He holds out to us. In the future, a sign of our faithfulness to God may not be found in efforts to recreate Christendom but instead among smaller, creative communities who can discern how God is working on the margins and gladly and contentedly participate in what emerges from the ground up, our expectations calibrated not to the past but to the images of the kingdom provided by Jesus Himself: salt, yeast and mustard seeds (see Matthew 5:13-16; 13:31-33). Each suggests something which is hidden and imperceptible to most but which slowly works upon that which is around it, adding flavour and bringing out the best in ways which are eventually found to be wonderfully transformative. And each reminds us that minority status is not something to be regarded as a failure for Christians, but something Jesus predicted. We are just as much the people of the house fellowships and the catacombs as we are the people of the cathedrals and the megachurches.

Finding our place in a new landscape

I can't remember why we took out a subscription but every month a copy of the consumer magazine *Which* arrives in the post, each issue offering comparisons and reviews of products and services available in the UK. Once a year, the magazine publishes a list of the best supermarkets in the country, its conclusions based on feedback from its many readers. The result of the most recent poll makes for interesting reading.[9] The shops that are most likely to be recommended to a friend are either those run by premium and prestigious brands, or those operated by newcomers to the British market who put value for money at the heart of their offering

That might seem like a surprising result to many of us. We might be wondering what happened to the famous household names that dominated the UK market for many years. However, the survey reflects a trend which many of us will recognise, what's sometimes referred to as 'the squeezed middle' of retailing.[10] Consumers have opted for either the quality offered by more expensive shops, or the value for money which can be found at the other end of the market. The retail sector is not the only one which has been affected by these sorts of changes. In recent years the automotive industry has changed significantly, as premium German manufacturers have produced smaller models which offer sophistication and quality to family-car buyers, while huge gains in market share have also been made by value brands such as those from Korea, all at the expense of previously dominant firms

I wonder if we're beginning to see similar changes take place in the British church landscape. In most towns and cities, there continue to be large, well-resourced congregations which are attended by middle-class members who can afford to give the sums of money which are needed to offer a well-resourced standard of church. Such churches can offer not only the services of a pastor, but also children's and youth workers, perhaps even administrators and paid worship leaders. Those attending may be money-rich and time-poor, unable to contribute much to church life themselves but able at least to provide the level of financial support needed to run programmes and projects to a high standard.

At the opposite end of the spectrum are the growing numbers of small communities of faith, for whom the focal point of the week may be a Friday-evening meal instead of a Sunday-morning worship service. Such communities will often value relationship to each other and to their neighbourhood more than programmes and provide a gathering place for those seeking faith alongside some who feel worn out or disillusioned by more traditional models of church.

Extending further our analogy from the marketplace, we might ask who the squeezed middle are in this scenario? Could it be that they are the majority of medium-sized congregations who are slowly declining but still able to employ at least one member of staff, usually a pastor, and who are doing their best to sustain programmes which are comparable to those of larger churches: gathered worship on a Sunday, Sunday and midweek youth and children's work, a variety of home groups alongside various forms of social outreach? However, running such a range of activities at the standard expected by many church attendees requires a level of professionalism and commitment which puts strains on many congregations. Think, for example, of the preparation for just one Sunday gathering: coffee and tea to be served, songs to be selected and rehearsed, PowerPoint to be assembled, sound and projection desks to be operated, a sermon to be written, helpers to be found (and DBS-checked) to work with children and young people. How many 'sabbaths' are actually more tiring than the other six days of labour as a consequence of these demands? Is it any wonder that many churches run the risk of being overwhelmed by the burden of their programmes?

How might some of the tensions highlighted in this chapter be resolved? One practical answer might be an honest reassessment of the level of activity undertaken by many of our churches. Starting a new activity is so much easier than closing an old one. The end of any church organisation is often taken as a sign of decline or defeat, but Jesus Himself affirmed that one thing ending is often that which creates the circumstances in which new life emerges: 'unless a grain of wheat falls into the earth and dies, it remains just a single grain; but if it dies, it bears much fruit' (John 12:24, NRSV). If some of our churches were willing to trade in their very busy programmes, in exchange for doing a few things well and creating more time in which to rest and deepen relationships, they might be surprised by the new vitality and energy which would emerge. We have grown used to the notion that those who are 'stepping out of the boat' are the ones who are always launching grand new projects. Perhaps we ought to give more recognition to those who demonstrate discipline in knowing the one thing they are called to do and sticking to it.

What I learned one Saturday morning

A final thought on how we measure our success comes from an unlikely source, a recent gathering with a few hundred other people, some friends and some strangers. We enjoyed conversation together before we shared the activity that provided the purpose for our gathering. And afterwards nobody rushed away so we stayed on and shared cake and coffee while catching up on the events of the last week.

This will probably sound like a familiar activity to many of us, except that the event I'm referring to isn't church. Instead it was my first experience of Parkrun, a remarkable story which began fifteen years ago when a group of friends gathered to share a run and then a coffee and which now has 250,000 participants in twenty countries. There are lots of lessons which churches could learn from Parkrun, not least the warm and non-judgemental welcome which is offered to people from all backgrounds and at all levels of ability. The events are also strikingly accessible. All you need to take part is a pair of running shoes and a printed barcode (there is no Parkrun app, in fact the whole event has a refreshingly low-tech feel). But there's one particular statistic which stands out in the Parkrun story.

Each week Parkrun gives everyone taking part the opportunity to run five kilometres. In 2005, the average time taken to complete a run was twenty-two minutes and sixteen seconds, but by 2017 it had risen to twenty-nine minutes and six seconds.[11] Parkrun organisers are apparently delighted at this statistic, which may seem strange at first. Why, after all, would any movement of runners be pleased that their participants are getting slower year on year? Parkrun's perspective is different. To them, this is evidence that they're making space for more and more people who have never run before, just the sort of people they want to attract.

What lessons might this story offer for our churches? How might our perspectives change if, instead of focusing on the number of people walking through our doors, we focused on their profile instead? It might seem strange to describe as a success a church with statistically fewer people who are mature followers of Jesus but surely this would be a sign of a church making room for outsiders, the sort of people He spent time with Himself.

For discussion

1. Consider again Jesus' words to Peter in John 21:20-22. How do they challenge our tendency to compare ourselves and our churches with what others are doing?
2. What benefits have you gained from the ministries of online preachers or worship leaders and what are the risks of focusing on them at the expense of what is happening in our local churches?
3. Read again the story of Hananiah and Jeremiah, found in Jeremiah 28. If one person is warning of judgement and loss and another is telling us God can help us overcome, how do we know who's right? How can we be sure which voices to listen to and which to be wary of?
4. What other influences can you think of which are preventing your church from facing up to the reality of its present situation?
5. What difference would it make to your local church if you only focused on a few ministries you think God

has equipped you for? What barriers exist to prevent you from getting to this place?

Notes

[1] Original source unknown.

[2] http://www.independent.co.uk/news/media/hello-magazine-celebrates-its-20th-birthday-824252.html (accessed 5th July 2019).

[3] I am grateful for this insight from Ian Stackhouse, offered at a Heart of England Baptist Association event in Birmingham in November 2014.

[4] Rick Warren, *The Purpose Driven Church* (Grand Rapids, MI: Zondervan, 1995).

[5] Richard Bauckham and Trevor Hart, *Finding God in the Midst of Life: Old Stories for Contemporary Readers* (Milton Keynes: Paternoster, 2006) p.25.

[6] Attributed to Peter de Vries, see https://www.goodreads.com/quotes/7211704-nostalgia-ain-t-what-it-used-to-be (accessed 29th July 2019).

[7] Examples include Walter Brueggemann, *Cadences of Home* (Louisville, KY: Westminster John Knox Press, 1997); Walter Brueggemann, *Out of Babylon* (Nashville, TN: Abingdon, 2010); Michael Frost, *Exiles* (Peabody, MA: Hendrickson, 2006).

[8] See John Goldingay, *Jeremiah for Everyone* (London: SPCK, 2015), p 141.

[9] Details of the survey can be found at: https://www.which.co.uk/reviews/supermarkets/article/best-and-worst-supermarkets/supermarkets-compared (accessed 29th July 2019).

[10] See, for example,
https://www.theguardian.com/commentisfree/2014/mar/13/supermarkets-squeezed-middle (accessed 5th July 2019).
[11] https://www.theguardian.com/sport/blog/2018/oct/01/parkrun-five-mlllion-runners (accessed 5th July 2019).

Chapter Three
The Gap between Activism and Trust

I spent eight years of my ministry on the outskirts of Birmingham, leading a church on one of the many estates than run along the southern edge of the city. Like many such areas in British cities, a frequent problem during that time was what could be diplomatically described as the 'antisocial' use of motorbikes and quad bikes. It was a daily occurrence to hear the drone of a two-stroke engine, shortly afterwards accompanied by the image of one or two bikes performing various stunts at high speed on either roads or pavements. The noise generated by these machines and the fear of a dreadful accident resulting from them being ridden in this way understandably became an issue of great concern in the community. Eventually, having listened to many people speak of the fear and distress they were experiencing, I decided it was time to contact some local leaders to see what could be done about the issue.

So it was that I found myself sitting in my office talking to two officers from our local neighbourhood team about the matter in hand. Policing an issue like this is notoriously difficult, as officers factor in concerns for their own safety and that of the public and bike riders. I'd expected a conversation about how I could support efforts to secure more resources to tackle this problem, but instead the ball was placed back in my court. One officer spoke about how impressed he'd been by his recent experience of Street Pastors in the city centre before asking, 'What can the churches do about this issue?'

There then followed one of those moments when several ideas race through your mind as you try to find a form of words to fill the silence. I thought about how our church could possibly find the volunteers to support yet another activity to meet needs in our community, given our existing commitments to an education project, a drop-in service and a foodbank. I wondered what our members were supposed to do, when faced with the prospect of a quad bike careering towards them at high speed. I found myself torn between the pressures generated by another request for help and my anxiety about failing to offer a solution on this occasion with all the signals such a response might send out about our concern for the needs of the community.

Since that conversation, I've reflected further on the assumptions which lay behind the question raised by the police about the respective roles and responsibilities of our organisations. Paul told the Roman Christians, 'The authorities that exist have been established by God … the one in authority is God's servant for your good' (Romans 13:1-4), and he also encouraged Timothy to pray 'for kings and all those in authority, that we may live peaceful and quiet lives in all godliness and holiness' (1 Timothy 2:2).

We are presented here with a perspective which appears to distinguish clearly between which jobs belong to the church and which are to be undertaken by the ruling authorities.

In recent years, however, these boundary lines have become increasingly blurred. The growing numbers of foodbanks, job clubs and debt-advice centres bear testimony to British churches' greater commitment to meet the need of the most vulnerable people in their communities. The reasons for this growth are probably twofold: firstly, the urgency of providing such help has been intensified by the benefit reductions introduced as part of the government austerity agenda implemented since 2010; secondly, the change reflects a recovery of a broader understanding of the gospel which evangelicals arguably lost in the first half of the twentieth century, a key moment being the agreement of the 1974 Lausanne Covenant which affirmed 'that evangelism and socio-political involvement are both part of our Christian duty'.[1] Most of us will now agree with the often-quoted truism, 'People don't care how much you know until they know how much you care'.

But is there a danger that we are losing a sense of discipline about what we are, and are not, called to do? How many local churches are now at the point of being overwhelmed by the needs of their community, feeling obliged to respond (and be seen to respond) meaningfully to every problem which presents itself? Is it always appropriate that we take on the running of the local library, post office or community centre? In many communities, churches are likely to offer the most readily available supply of volunteer energy and skills, as well as meeting space, making them the first port of call for local authorities keen to establish new projects or sustain existing services.

How can we find a healthy balance between activism and the service of others, and giving time and space to the reflective, contemplative practices which are also necessary for our spiritual formation? In this chapter, we'll consider this question, learning from the experiences of previous generations of believers.

Taking the long view

Foodbanks… parish nursing… parenting classes… it's all too easy to look at the wide array of social projects offered by many congregations and assume that we are more socially engaged than any of our predecessors. But if we take just a cursory look at ministries of previous generations, we soon find ourselves standing in a tradition stretching back further than many of us might have realised.

This was a generation of Christian philanthropists who offered leadership to a range of social improvements in a time when such tasks were not yet seen as the responsibility of the state. Services led by the church included Sunday schools and unendowed schools which provided discipline and basic skills in literacy to more than 1 million students in their heyday.[2] For those working long hours in the factories which were appearing everywhere during the Industrial Revolution, these church-based schools offered a precious opportunity for learning and advancement. The size and scope of such projects was often impressive. In 1836, for example, Cannon Street Baptist Church in Birmingham had 591 pupils attending school, with a Sick Club which offered home tuition to ill students.[3]

Another important ministry offered by Victorian churches was visiting. The vast majority of this work was undertaken by women, who were regarded as having a better understanding of domestic affairs and who could freely call on homes during the day when men were often at work, offering advice on issues such as food, clothing, parenting and hygiene.[4]

Again, the scale of this voluntary work was genuinely impressive. In 1889, for example, the Church of England calculated that it had 47,112 district visitors in England and Wales, a figure that rose to 74,009 by 1910.[5] Further support was provided by the 'mothers' meetings' which offered a combination of biblical reflections and training in such practical skills as needlework[6] and nursing, which enabled the poor to access a rudimentary level of medical care.[7]

It's hard not to be impressed and humbled by the service these Victorian churches offered their communities. However, we need to reflect on two aspects of this story which I think offer a lesson for our current situation.

Firstly, the extensive work undertaken in these ministries did not result in significant increases in church attendance. To raise this point is not to detract from the value of the work undertaken, but rather to highlight how it failed to break down social divisions, including those between the poor and the middle-class Christians who emphasised values such as sobriety and hard work. Those who experienced poverty were unable to afford the respectable 'Sunday best' attire of other church attenders, and were also put off by practices such as the need in some churches to rent pews.[8] One 'solution' to this problem was the setting-up of mission halls, designed to be more accessible than more established congregations but regarded by many as a poor substitute.

Most of us no longer wear hats to church, and many of our pews have now been replaced by more comfortable and flexible seating arrangements. But what barriers exist today which limit the participation of marginalised people in our churches? How many might feel like their clothes don't bear comparison to the Sunday best of others in the congregation? How many can make a connection between the struggles of their lives and the triumphal tone of the majority of modern worship songs? How many find it hard to receive hope or good news in a room set up like a classroom with a service that favours those who enjoy reading? We live in a time when our understanding of the need to be accessible will ensure large-print Bibles and a hearing-aid loop are made available, while failing to realise how many might be alienated by the layout of our sanctuaries and the format of our services.

A second lesson from the Victorian era of church activism can be learned when we consider how it ended. At the turn of the century, Seebohm Rowntree's famous book *Poverty: A Study of Town Life*[9] alerted the public to the shocking living conditions of the poor in York, bringing an understandable urgency to calls for better welfare provision.[10] Church leaders, increasingly convinced that the scale of change needed to lift large numbers of people out of dire poverty could not be brought about through piecemeal charitable deeds, played a prominent role in the campaign for greater government intervention.

It's been suggested that in advocating for better state education and welfare provision, churches were effectively putting themselves out of business, and thereby sowing the seeds of their own decline.[11] The reality was probably more complicated. Other significant changes were taking place in this era that also contributed to a decline in church membership: exciting new alternatives to church that included the attractions of music halls and then the cinema, and new sports such as football and cricket. Some churches began a fightback against such distractions, including Baptist congregations who offered less formal activities under the wonderfully quaint title of 'Pleasant Sunday Afternoons'.[12]

However, it's still hard to escape the impression that churches were struggling to define their role in the early twentieth century, as the state assumed responsibility for so much that they had previously done. And this raises important questions for our churches. For now, there seems to be no sign of the demand slowing down for the foodbanks, debt counselling and many other social ministries offered by churches. But will the era of austerity last forever? What will happen when the tide turns and there is no longer an expectation that churches meet these needs? What will be left of our relationships with our local communities when they are no longer dependent on us for running services on their behalf?

When we're faced with so many pressing needs, our immediate instinct can be that actions and not words are the only valid response. But a number of key moments in the ministry of Jesus seem to warn us against this presumption. One of the temptations He faced was using His power to 'tell these stones to become bread' (Matthew 4:3). Such a miracle could have drawn a huge following from the vast majority of people living in first-century Palestine for whom subsistence was a way of life. His reply to the tempter is telling: 'Man shall not live on bread alone, but on every word that comes from the mouth of God' (Matthew 4:4).

Of course, there are several occasions when we do find Jesus responding to the physical needs of people. John 6 records one such incident, the Feeding of the Five Thousand, when Jesus realises the need to provide food for the large number of people who have gathered to hear His teaching. The following day the same crowds come after Jesus again, apparently looking for a repeat of the same event. When they eventually catch up with Him, Jesus offers a penetrating insight into their motivations, while also encouraging them to look beyond the satisfaction that comes from having their physical hunger met:

> Very truly I tell you, you are looking for me, not because you saw the signs I performed but because you ate the loaves and had your fill. Do not work for food that spoils, but for food that endures to eternal life, which the Son of Man will give you.
> *John 6:26-27*

Later in the same conversation, He famously says of Himself, 'I am the bread of life. Whoever comes to me will never go hungry, and whoever believes in me will never be thirsty' (John 6:35). Jesus recognised that there are moments when love requires an immediate response to a human need, but in this conversation with the crowd He displays a determined discipline about the deeper purpose of His mission, an understanding that He cannot allow Himself to always be distracted by short-term problem-solving.

We find a similar pattern when we consider the instructions Jesus gave His disciples about how the message of the kingdom was to be proclaimed. As He sends out the twelve in Matthew 10, He famously tells them:

> As you go, proclaim this message: 'The kingdom of heaven has come near.' Heal those who are ill, raise the dead, cleanse those who have leprosy, drive out demons. Freely you have received; freely give.
> *Matthew 10:7-8*

The good news which is to be broadcast is astonishingly significant, nothing less than the declaration that a new era has begun, the long-promised rule of God has broken into the world and makes possible the healing and liberation of all who find their lives damaged and distorted by the effects of the fall.[13] The message is made visible in miraculous acts which demonstrate how the kingdom pushes back against the old order, enabling the healing of those who are sick and rendered unworthy in others' eyes as a consequence, allowing the release of those who are trapped in destructive habits and patterns. Most wonderfully, it is seen in the raising to life in situations where the greatest enemy of all, death, seems to have prevailed. And yet these deeds, in and of themselves, are not enough. There is also something to be said, a word to be announced. 'As you go, proclaim …'

In discussions on contemporary mission, a phrase is often quoted which is invariably attributed to Francis of Assisi: 'Preach the gospel at all times. If necessary use words.' Pithy, quotable (and tweetable) though it may be, this sentiment is misleading and unhelpful, setting up an unnecessary tension between words and deeds and causing us to think of what we say as inherently inferior to activity.[14] As we look at the story of Jesus, we find Him providing for us with the ultimate example of how this is lived out, His words and His actions constantly interpreting each other. Luke's Gospel offers several examples of this principle. A sermon about the importance of loving enemies is best understood in light of the healing of a centurion's servant (Luke 6:27-36 and 7:1-10). The welcome which is offered to a sinful woman who gatecrashes a meal at Simon the Pharisee's house makes more sense as we hear words which command us not to look for the speck in our neighbour's eye (Luke 6:37-42 and 7:36-50). It's one thing to be told of the need to build our lives on firm foundations, and another to read the story of a man held so firmly in the grip of his possessions that he cannot do what Jesus asks of him in order to inherit eternal life (Luke 6:46-49 and 18:18-30).

There's no doubt that, when it comes to deeds which demonstrate the values of the kingdom, many local churches are doing more than ever before. But could it be that there's a sense in which the make-up of so many of these projects is robbing us of our confidence in the difference we can make in our everyday conversations? Alongside the work of many congregations who are seeking to help the marginalised, we have also seen the growth in recent years of a new industry, parachurch organisations offering a variety of models and franchises which enable churches to establish new projects. Often these groups can offer valuable insights to churches based on the experience they've acquired, as well as training and guidelines on policy and procedures. However, the effect of such tightly regulated models can often be as disempowering to local churches as it is enabling, with a risk that the focus quickly shifts from meeting human need to ensuring that the manual is being properly followed, and more of a debate is needed about the way in which some organisations are loading on to local churches the risks and resource requirements which enable their own expansion.

Our congregations are full of people with compassion, a desire to serve others and insights and wisdom to offer from a lifetime's experience of work, raising children and following Jesus. Why do they need to pay for someone to tell them how to run a group that enables fathers to spend time with young children, or give them a logo and branding to prove their ability to make a Christmas hamper for their neighbours? The effect of these encounters can sometimes be to turn natural, caring human interactions into tightly regulated processes, the impression being given that there's only one way to support someone in need and it's only the experts who can tell us what it looks like.

If we're constantly preoccupied with initiatives which are driven from above, it becomes harder for us to see what is happening below, to appreciate the power of everyday conversations and encounters. What might change if we understood that we don't need to be participants in a project to act kindly towards others, that compassionate deeds still matter even if they can't be accounted for in the statistics of a social enterprise? We live in a culture which designates value through data, causing us to believe that activities only count when there are measurable outcomes which can be logged. How many food parcels delivered? How many clients visited? The effect of all of this is to cause us to worry that God is only using us on the occasions when there is evidence which can clearly be logged. We lose sight of the seeds He may be sowing in our lives because we obsess over counting that which is being reaped.

Taking it slowly

A possibly apocryphal tale has it that Pope John XXIII was once asked how we should behave in the scenario that Jesus was returning. He is said to have replied with just two words: 'Look busy!'[15] If this is really what Jesus is looking for, one suspects that He would not be disappointed by many members of our churches. One of the most striking aspects of modern church life is the sheer volume of activity often undertaken by a small and committed core of a congregation. Given that most churches find it easier to begin projects than close them down, it is hardly surprising that in many cases the busyness seems to grow year on year. And with the launch of the latest must-have evangelistic tool or denominational initiative we find ourselves feeling the need to add an extra commitment into our programmes.

But could it be the case that what passes for passion in some of our churches is actually a form of anxiety, our activities driven by a concern over declining numbers and finances or rising age profiles, all of which cause to us to feel that 'something must be done'? Of course, 'There is a time for everything' (Ecclesiastes 3:1): there will be occasions when it's appropriate for us to pursue innovative strategies for growth, but we need also to be wary of losing sight of the value of practices which have been the means by which disciples have been formed for 2,000 years in which the gates of hell have not yet prevailed against the church:[16] passages of Scripture read, peace shared, bread broken and wine consumed, prayers and liturgies rehearsed. As we gather to share these practices, we may experience them as routine, even presuming that little significant change has occurred in our lives on some occasions. But slowly, steadily, gradually, we find these to be the means used by God to transform our habits and thinking.

Near the end of his second letter, the apostle Peter offers final words of encouragement to the early believers to whom he is writing:

The Lord is not slow in keeping his promise, as some understand slowness. Instead he is patient with you, not wanting anyone to perish, but everyone to come to repentance.

2 Peter 3:9

These few lines shed light on an aspect of God's character which seems strikingly at odds with the frenetic pace of church life described above. Maybe, deep down, some of us might even consider this patience to be a slightly inappropriate response in light of all the pressing needs our world is facing. Perhaps we feel we know better than the God who decided to take a rest after six days of creation (Genesis 2:2-3) or the Saviour whose three years of ministry were punctuated by frequent withdrawal to quiet places in order to pray (Luke 5:16). God asks no more of His people than He has done Himself when commanding Sabbath (Exodus 20:8-11), a weekly cessation of activity that extends even to animals.

The Jewish understanding of Sabbath is that of a time which is tangibly different from any other, a day characterised by the cessation of the activities which crowd and press in for the other six days of the week.[17]

What is described here feels so far removed from the experience many contemporary Christians might have of Sunday, our own 'day of rest' often becoming the busiest of our week. In a world where so many people are exhausted, working longer hours than ever, it is hard to see how this activity is in any way countercultural.

In recent years, a number of writers have contrasted the busyness of our present church programmes with the virtue of patience and its importance for the early church.[18] Many of these believers lived with the constant threat of violent persecution and were invariably a minority in the cultures in which they lived.

It's important to stress that their belief in the importance of patience did not lead to inertia or a piety which failed to recognise the needs of outsiders. These early Christians gained the respect and admiration of others on account of their care for the poor and destitute. They also grew steadily in spite of having an approach to evangelism which differs markedly from our contemporary 'seeker-friendly' strategies. Outsiders were made welcome only after persuading church leaders that they were teachable and taking seriously their enquiry into following Jesus, an understandable practice for a church wary of infiltration by spies. The overriding impression of the church in these early centuries is a movement whose growth was not the result of a missional strategy, but rather the natural by-product of a commitment to discipleship which affected every aspect of behaviour.

Unlike us, these early Christians were not blessed with large buildings or cash reserves, and nor was their thinking affected by a desire to gain influence or win respect from wider society. They were not in a hurry.

In a wonderful reflection on the speed at which God works, the Japanese theologian Kosuke Koyama notes that

> God walks slowly because he is love. If he is not love he would have gone much faster. Love has its speed. It is an inner speed. It is a spiritual speed. It is a different kind of speed from the technological speed to which we are accustomed. It is 'slow' yet it

is lord over all other speeds since it is the speed of love.[19]

God's purposes are driven by His love, not by targets or timetables. Corporate recovery programmes and five-year plans may work well in industry, but it still surprises me when churches adopt them, as if we can dictate terms to God about the timetable on which He is to work and compel Him to perform in certain ways as and when we see fit.

When the apostle Paul wrote to the Corinthian Christians and listed the many qualities associated with love, it is telling that he first noted that 'Love is patient ...' (1 Corinthians 13:4). Love moves forward inch by inch, with a desire that every possible opportunity will be offered for the object of its affection to draw closer in relationship. 'It does not insist on its own way' (1 Corinthians 13:5, NRSV). It will not impose deadlines or dictate terms. 'It bears all things, believes all things, hopes all things, endures all things' (1 Corinthians 13:7, NRSV). Love is willing to look beyond an aspiration for immediate results: it trusts that in the long-term 'all shall be well and all manner of things shall be well'.[20]

Of course, patience is not an excuse for failing to act. As those words from Peter remind us, God does not want 'anyone to perish, but everyone to come to repentance' (2 Peter 3:9). His love and patience do not manifest themselves in passive inaction. His Spirit is endlessly at work, alerting people to His love and seeking to welcome them into the wholeness and freedom which are His best for everyone. Perhaps we would relax more and exhaust ourselves less if we remembered that it is not up to us to begin every new initiative but rather to discern where God is already at work so that we can follow and be part of it.

It is hard to do this if we are constantly looking over our shoulder, concerned with numbers or feeling the need to address every social problem or shortfall in resources in our community. If we want to be attractive to others, a good place to start would be to recognise the danger of limitless service. We work, and then, like God, we recognise that a time comes to stop working, that creation and new creation can survive without our activity. We breathe easy, we relax, we assume a quiet confidence in our loving Father to solve in His time the problems which are beyond us.

For discussion

1. Do you agree with the suggestion that some of our churches are at risk of being exhausted or distracted by social action? What do you see as the warning signs that a congregation may be doing too much?
2. Consider again the balance between the words spoken by Jesus and the way He acted to live these words out. How does this contrast with the mixture of words and deeds in your own church's approach to mission?
3. What do you see as the benefits and risks of using models developed by other charities for the projects by which we serve our local communities?
4. How does your experience of Sunday compare with the description of the Jewish Sabbath found in this chapter? Can you think of any practical steps you or

your church could take to make Sunday more of a day of rest?

5. What would you say to someone who complained that being patient is just an excuse for doing nothing?

Notes

[1] https://www.lausanne.org/content/covenant/lausanne-covenant#cov (accessed 11th July 2019).

[2] See Frank Prochaska, *Christianity and Social Service in Modern Britain: The Disinherited Spirit* (Oxford: OUP, 2006), p 148.

[3] A Betteridge, *Deep Roots, Living Branches: A History of Baptists in the English Western Midlands* (Leicester: Matador, 2010), p 152.

[4] See Prochaska, *Christianity and Social Service in Modern Britain*, p 68.

[5] Ibid, p 65.

[6] Ibid, pp 98-122.

[7] Ibid, pp 124-127.

[8] See Betteridge, *Deep Roots, Living Branches*, p 357.

[9] Benjamin Seebohm Rowntree, *Poverty: A Study of Town Life* (London: Macmillan, 1901).

[10] See Andrew Marr, *The Making of Modern Britain* (London: Macmillan, 2009), pp 16-22.

[11] See Prochaska, *Christianity and Social Service in Modern Britain*, p 151.

[12] See Betteridge, *Deep Roots, Living Branches*, p 331.

[13] Genesis 3.

[14] It's also important to note that while this phrase is frequently attributed to Francis, there is actually no record of him ever having said such a thing. In fact, as Mark Galli notes, 'Francis was known as much for his preaching as for his lifestyle',

which makes it all the more implausible that he would have expressed this view. See http://www.christianitytoday.com/ct/2009/mayweb-only/120-42.0.html (accessed 5th July 2019).

[15] https://www.thinkingfaith.org/articles/20111220_1.htm (accessed 5th July 2019).

[16] See Matthew 16:18.

[17] See Ruth Haley Barton, *Sacred Rhythms* (Grand Rapids, MI: Zondervan, 2011), p 136.

[18] Notable examples include Alan Kreider, *The Patient Ferment of the Early Church* (Grand Rapids, MI: Baker Academic, 2016) and C Christopher Smith and John Pattison, *Slow Church: Cultivating Community in the Patient Way of Jesus* (Downers Grove, IL: IVP USA, 2014).

[19] Kosuke Koyama, *Three Mile an Hour God* (Maryknoll, NY: Orbis, 1979), p 7.

[20] These words are attributed to Julian of Norwich. See https://www.christianhistoryinstitute.org/incontext/article/julian/ (accessed 5th July 2019).

Chapter Four
The Gap between Doing For and Being With

I spent ten years of my life as a commuter. Each weekday morning I would leave our home in Exeter and spend thirty minutes driving along what locals called 'the valley road', the beautiful A396 which runs parallel to the River Exe. From nine to five, I worked for a financial information provider in the town of Tiverton. Despite the many hours I spent at a desk in an industrial estate on the outskirts of the town, it was a place I barely got to know. Occasionally, I would drive into town for lunch with a colleague and I remember when some of us spent an evening sampling the delights of grass-roots football at Tiverton Town. But most of my time was spent in the office, answering emails, attending meetings or joining in conference calls with colleagues in such places as New York, Singapore and Bangalore.

And then, at the end of the day, I would drive home. While I often spent the journey to work preoccupied with the tasks I had to attend to, the journey back was a welcome time to unwind, Friday evenings a particular highlight as the weekend began with Mark Lawrenson previewing football fixtures on Radio Five Live. That half-hour became a valued part of each day, time when I could put some distance between myself and my work and return home having unwound from the pressures of the day job. Evenings during the week and Saturdays and Sundays could be spent in a different place, without the risk of running unexpectedly into colleagues and being reminded of the demands which would be placed upon me when I next returned to the office.

As we discovered earlier, the increasing availability of personal transport from the second half of the twentieth century has dramatically transformed the way we relate to our communities. We can work at a place removed from where we live. We're no longer restricted to buying our groceries at the corner shop when it's possible to choose which out-of-town supermarket to shop in (or which online retailer to order from). We don't need to spend an evening at the local pub when we can climb into the car and drive to a restaurant or cinema.

And nor do we need to worship at our local church. We may feel that what's on offer just around the corner from us isn't exactly to our taste: perhaps it's too high or too low. It could be that there aren't enough children in the Sunday school so we wonder how our own family would fit in. Maybe we feel that there aren't enough 'people like us' with whom we have a sense of connection. We might baulk at the church's stance on some theological issue, feeling they're too welcoming or not welcoming enough to a particular group of people. Perhaps we tried the local church for a while but we had a disagreement with someone or didn't like the new minister, or felt that God was calling us to worship somewhere else. If that's the case, we can easily climb into the car and travel to the congregation a few miles down the road which does provide what we're looking for, a task made all the easier for us when it seems the array of choices available to us is wider than ever.

I realise, of course, that there are some situations when someone remaining at a church becomes unsustainable, when so much pain or disappointment lingers that it's best for parties to go their separate ways or when the unity of a congregation is threatened because there is such a wide divergence of opinion. But, if we're honest with ourselves, our motivations for moving can often be more to do with the allure of the greener grass on the other side of the fence. Sustaining relationships in any church can be hard work, so it's not surprising that we sometimes feel attracted by the possibility of a fresh start elsewhere, even though we may find ourselves confronted, sooner or later, with the same problems as before, given that they often concern our own hearts and hang-ups rather than those of others in our congregation.

In an interview conducted a few years before his death, the pastor and theologian Eugene Peterson was asked what advice he would offer to younger Christians who are looking for 'a deeper and more authentic discipleship'. His advice is telling:

> Go to the nearest smallest church and commit yourself to being there for 6 months. If it doesn't work out, find somewhere else. But don't look for programs, don't look for entertainment, and don't look for a great preacher. A Christian congregation

is not a glamorous place, not a romantic place. That's what I always told people. If people were leaving my congregation to go to another place of work, I'd say, 'The smallest church, the closest church, and *stay there* for 6 months.' Sometimes it doesn't work. Some pastors are just incompetent. And some are flat out bad. So I don't think that's the answer to everything, but it's a better place to start than going to the one with all the programs, the glitz, all that stuff.[1]

Peterson is the author of numerous books on theology and pastoral leadership, but he's probably best known as the author/translator of the paraphrase, *The Message*. One of my favourite interpretations of a passage in this work is Peterson's rendering of John 1:14. Describing the way in which Jesus came to earth and lived among us, John uses a word which would have been loaded with significance for his first readers: *skēnoō* literally means to 'pitch a tent', and was the same word used in the Greek version of the Old Testament, the Septuagint, to communicate the idea of the tabernacle, the portable 'dwelling place' carried by the people of Israel at the time of the Exodus, a physical reminder of the presence of God among them. Peterson powerfully conveys the full force of the concept of 'tabernacle' in his translation of John:

> The Word became flesh and blood,
> and moved into the neighborhood.
> We saw the glory with our own eyes,
> the one-of-a-kind glory,
> like Father, like Son,

Generous inside and out,
true from start to finish.
John 1:14 (The Message)

The idea of 'moving in' is one of the major themes of John's Gospel, the Word arriving from the 'world above' and entering into the 'world below'. One world is characterised by the qualities of light, truth and life, in contrast to the darkness, lies and deadness which keep people trapped and lost and apart from God. This idea of physical presence, of dwelling in a particular place among a particular people, is integral to the Christian idea of how God saves us. Jesus walked and talked, worked and rested, laughed and cried among a group of friends, relationships formed in the villages and towns of first-century Palestine. It's a far cry from our contemporary situation, when there are so often gaps to be bridged between the places where we live, work and worship.

Commuter worship: causes and consequences

At this point we need to acknowledge the glaring differences between our own culture and the world inhabited by Jesus. Ours is a mobile society with many of us enjoying access to personal and private transport that our forebears could only have dreamed of. We also need to acknowledge the impact of technology on our relationships. We now live in a networked world, where some of our most important connections might be those formed and sustained on social media.

Conversely, however, we are encountering new barriers to mobility which didn't confront previous generations. For example, many of the houses which immediately surround the congregation where I currently live are unaffordable for most young families. Some of those who grew up in our church and want to continue to worship with us discover that it's not always possible to get accommodation nearby.

The phrase 'redemption and lift' was first used by church growth expert Donald McGavran in the 1970s.[2] This theory suggests that the order and self-discipline which Christian faith can bring leads to economic and social advancement for followers, thereby preventing them from sharing faith with those from the marginalised communities where they previously lived. McGavran applied this idea primarily to Christians in the developing world, observing that it holds true not only for individuals but also whole movements which can struggle to sustain growth once a pioneer generation gives way to a more established and well-resourced church. However, he also noted its relevance to the church in the West, where congregations in areas of deprivation are often numerically smaller than nearby middle-class ones. It's tempting to consider how this theory might be applied today, in estate churches which are led by people who grew up in the area but have since moved to the adjoining suburbs as they benefited from educational and career opportunities. They may still share a heart for the places where they worship while failing to see how they no longer share the same values, and how their new-found status and wealth will place an inevitable distance between them and those to whom their churches are reaching out.

In many cases, leadership in poorer churches will still be the preserve of the middle class. I am not doubting the sincerity and commitment of those who serve in this way, and it also needs to be recognised that the important role they play is a reflection of the increasing regulation that churches now need to comply with (for example, Charity Commission rules, safeguarding, health and safety legislation), creating an environment where leaders need to be able to negotiate more complex processes that are less daunting for those with professional experience. But we also need to acknowledge and recognise the difficulty of understanding the assets and needs of a community where we don't live, the joys and frustrations experienced by local residents. There's a difference to our worship when it's alongside the people we bump into during the week. There's an added edge to our prayers when they give expression to events which have taken place in the streets near the church and which are common knowledge to those in the community.

Issues of justice are also at stake here. In many communities, some of the clearest delineators of power are between those who feel forced to stay and those who have the resources to move away, between those who can afford to travel out of the area and those who know nothing more than the boundary lines of the estate, or between those who struggle to survive and those who can acquire resources to protect themselves from pain or inconvenience.

Roy McCloughry has noted that the mobility of our modern society often prevents us from building close relationships with our neighbours (why bother if we are only passing through?) and stops us from feeling responsible for areas where we do not expect to live for long.[3] As we'll discover in a moment, churches are not the only institutions to have been affected by such changes in recent years, but we need to acknowledge our own complicity before considering the bigger picture.

The rise of the middle classes

'Rochester!' Say the name, and to some you'll merely conjure up the thought of a historic market town in Kent. But for Labour Party activists of a nervous disposition, the phrase will be enough to send shivers down the spine, evoking painful memories of an incident which provides a salutary reminder of why those who tweet in haste may well end up repenting at leisure. During the November 2014 by-election campaign, shadow attorney general Emily Thornberry famously posted on social media a photo of a white van parked outside a house bedecked with two English flags. Within days Thornberry had resigned following heavy criticism of what many regarded as the snobbery implicit in her tweet, which provoked soul-searching among some in the party about the extent to which it had moved away from its working-class roots.

The emergence of Labour as a political force was one of the most monumental developments in British political life in the twentieth century. There were obvious benefits for the poor which arose from the provision of state housing and better schools and insurance, but also new challenges as their lives came to be, effectively, supervised by the government. An example of this loss of autonomy can be seen as early as the 1920s with the rules introduced for new council homes being built, strict regulations on how homes and gardens were to be maintained and prohibitions on keeping pigeons and poultry.[4]

The story of the British working class in the twentieth century is not just one of better welfare provision and living standards, a rising tide which saw many move from factory floors and mines to the safer, cleaner environs of the office or retail unit. For many, it has been a story of disempowerment, with government agencies playing an increasingly supervisory role in the lives of their citizens. The establishment of the welfare state set in motion a chain of events which has taken us to our current situation, where in many cases when the working class come into contact with the middle class it is in a context where the middle-class person is in some kind of supervisory capacity: the teacher of their child, their social worker or health visitor, or the kind church volunteer who is deciding what they will be eating as they pack their bags at the foodbank.

One of the saddest aspects of this history has been the way in which institutions which previously belonged to the working class and were a means of their self-improvement have been stolen from them. Church schools are now run by the government, friendly societies have morphed into major financial institutions and the Labour Party has come to be increasingly dominated by the middle class in an era of professionalised politics. Since the 1960s, Labour's quest for equality has taken it beyond the issue of rights for the working class. It has focused its energy on a progressive agenda which has enabled changes such as the decriminalisation of homosexuality, successive Race Relations Acts and the Equal Pay Act of 1970. I believe these are developments to be affirmed, yet these progressive values seem to have produced a party which sometimes appears disdainful of voters who are considered 'neither rich enough nor cultured enough'.[5]

And to this list of institutions becoming more remote from the working class we can add many of our churches. As Martyn Lloyd-Jones famously observed:

> Far too often, as nonconformist men have got on in the world, and made money and become Managers and Owners, they have become opponents of the working classes who were agitating for their rights.[6]

How should we respond to these developments? I am not suggesting that all middle-class Christians should walk away from the leadership roles they have in their churches, nor do I want to devalue the commitment with which they serve. However, I do believe we need a far deeper level of self-awareness about the ways in which we all bring assumptions and methods from our jobs and homes which then affect the culture of our churches in ways we might not even be aware of. Whether it's sitting on the committee of a political party, chairing the planning group for the community fun day, or leading a church, the fact is that belonging to the middle class equips someone with certain skills which inevitably mean that the organisations they lead take on their own image. We have standards and expectations about how events should be planned and publicised, what food or drink is needed for good hospitality, how publicity is written and produced... a variety of assumptions which change group cultures in ways we might not even be aware of, given that the language used and the methods employed are ones which we take as givens.

Twice in my life I've had the privilege of travelling overseas, once to Kenya and once to India, to meet with Christians in those countries and learn from them. On each occasion, I had training on the importance of cross-cultural mission, the need to be sensitive to the differences between my own background and experiences and the practices of those I would be visiting. I was taught what to wear and what not to wear. I was given advice on how to accept offers of food and drink. I have gained similar experiences as I've engaged in interfaith conversations in my role as a pastor. I know, for example, that when I visit the mosque it's important to take off my shoes, and I also know that when I'm the host there are certain foods which I would never serve because of the offence I would cause.

Most of us in twenty-first-century Britain have now learned to be sensitive to such ethnic and racial differences, and yet I wonder if the biggest cultural gaps of all are those between the working class and the middle class. The majority of us now have a greater appreciation of cultural diversity and understand how unacceptable it is to label others on the basis of their ethnicity or sexuality. But it could be argued that in recent years the most 'othered' group of people in our culture have been the poor, shamed in the media through 'poverty porn' such as Channel 4's *Benefits Street* and often portrayed as irresponsible by our political leaders. Our double standards about who counts and who doesn't is brilliantly summed up by the writer Owen Jones, as he describes a dinner party where one of the hosts tries to lighten the mood with a casual joke about 'chavs'. As Jones notes:

> Sitting around the table were people from more than one ethnic group. The gender split was fifty-fifty and not everyone was straight. All would have placed themselves left-of-centre politically. They would have bristled at being labelled a snob. If a stranger had attended that evening and disgraced him or herself by bandying around a word like 'Paki' or 'poof', they would have found themselves swiftly ejected from the flat.
>
> But no one flinched at a joke about chavs shopping in Woolies.[7]

The differences between our class and background reveal themselves in a variety of ways. Do we live for the present or do we plan for the future? Is our view of the world restricted to the local, or do we think, instead, in terms of networks? Are we motivated by the need to survive or a desire for achievement?[8] Our answers to these questions will reveal much about our background and social status, what we take for granted and our confidence about the control we have with regard to our prospects for the future.

One example of how class reveals itself in our churches can be found in some of the most popular enquirers' courses offered by British congregations. No one can deny the fruitfulness of such programmes as Alpha and Christianity Explored, which have been the means of many people coming to faith in our churches, but the course material presented often focuses on existential questions about the meaning of life, our identity and the ways in which we can discern God's guidance. Such issues are undoubtedly relevant for many of us but they matter far less to those who are simply trying to get by from one day to the next.

If we had a better understanding of the issues being faced by some of those on the margins of our society, we might run enquirers' courses which attempted to answer a different set of questions. How about conversations on themes such as: 'What does God think about injustice?', 'What is His message for the rich and the poor?', 'Does God believe in my potential?', 'How does my family compare to the ones described in the Bible and how was God working through them?'

Perhaps the most important question of all concerns where we have these conversations and on whose terms. Reading the accounts of His ministry in all four Gospels, it is striking to note how many occasions on which Jesus accepts hospitality from others. It is often harder to receive than give, to put ourselves in the uncomfortable position of being in someone else's space, letting them decide what we eat and allowing them to set the tone of the conversation. But this is what we often find Jesus doing: in Luke's Gospel, for example, He is the guest at the home of Levi the tax collector (Luke 5:27-32), Simon the Pharisee (where He allows Himself to be anointed by 'A woman in that town who lived a sinful life') (Luke 7:36-50), the home of Mary and Martha (Luke 10:38-42) and another tax collector, Zacchaeus (Luke 19:1-10). Often His teaching is in direct response to the questions of others: 'what must I do to inherit eternal life?' (Luke 10:25), 'Lord, are only a few people going to be saved?' (Luke 13:23), 'Once, on being asked by the Pharisees when the kingdom of God would come, Jesus replied ...' (Luke 17:20).

How might our approaches to mission change if we adopted this kind of approach? We might find the experience more humbling and generating a greater level of vulnerability than we're used to. There may be moments when we're confronted with our prejudices or even embarrassed by our naivety, as we're forced to consider answers to questions which haven't previously occurred to us. And we may also discover that the change God is asking of us goes further than how we communicate and challenges the very basis on which we're relating to others.

Power, privilege and charity

A recent poll by the UK Evangelical Alliance provides evidence of the increasing awareness many local churches now have of the importance of expressing kingdom values through care and provision for the poor and marginalised. Forty-four per cent of those surveyed said that 'their church works on a project to tackle poverty in their community' while 76 per cent agreed that 'local churches should organise themselves to share their God-given wealth so that none of their members experience poverty'.[9] The last decade has seen a proliferation of foodbanks, job clubs and debt advice centres which bears witness to British churches' increasing commitment to meet the needs of the most vulnerable people in their communities.[10] But is there a danger that these acts of service, offered from a place of greater wealth, might actually be placing more barriers between people, perpetuating divisions between 'them and us'? It might be that we think of ourselves as offering our help unconditionally and with grace, but can such interactions ever truly match the ideals we attach to them? How much time do we take to consider the toll which is taken on those who find themselves at the point where their only way forward is to be on the receiving end of our charity?

Reflecting on the basis on which we operate many of our social action projects takes us into the complex area of power and what to do with it. The instinctive response of many Christians might be to suggest that power can corrupt and seduce us and is therefore to be avoided, but the story of Scripture begins by offering a different perspective. At the beginning of Genesis, we read of God delegating authority to people who are given:

> dominion over the fish of the sea and over the birds
> of the air and over every living thing that moves
> upon the earth.
> *Genesis 1:28 (NRSV)*

What we discover here is a mandate to tame chaos and work to shape and transform the world, an uncompleted aspect of creation which is delegated to humans. Using the resources at our disposal to meet the needs of the vulnerable and needy could certainly be understood as a working out of this command.

But many of our churches and their members are in possession of not just power, but privilege, the accumulation of the opportunities and benefits which come the way of those who find life working largely on terms favourable to us. Many of us reading this book might not think of ourselves as particularly privileged, but maybe that's another aspect of the blindness of privilege. Privilege comes in many forms: our personal wealth and investments, our qualifications, even our social acquaintances. In a society where whom you know still matters as much as what you know, it's worth taking a moment to reflect on the wide network of connections available to the average church attender. How many work placements or summer internships have been facilitated by church connections? And in spite of decades of declining attendance, the church in the UK continues to be an institution with vast resources at its disposal in the form of investments and properties, many of which may be in need of repair but which offer significant floorspace in attractive locations.

The fact that so many of us approach our social projects from a position of privilege means that we all too often run the risk of what the American writer Andy Crouch describes as 'benevolent god playing'.[11]

It's instructive to reflect on this phrase, and then consider, for example, the interactions which take place at a church foodbank. If I help in such a setting, I will meet with 'clients', talking to them from the side of the desk which puts me in a position of power. I will ask them questions about whatever difficulties have resulted in them needing the help of this service, sometimes invasive enquiries which imply judgements (is it more or less shameful to need help because of debt, illness, benefit sanctions or funeral costs?). Then I will go and fetch the food, making decisions for someone else about what they will eat for the next few days. I may have helped that person in need, but without making myself vulnerable. I have disclosed nothing about myself and my own failings, and the conversation has probably created little space for the other person to share about their strengths and abilities. Sometimes it's easier to do something *for* someone than to spend time *with* them, to relate on the terms of our defined roles rather than person-to-person.

The early Church understood itself to be a place where social barriers were broken down as a new community was formed around the person of Jesus. In his letter to the Galatians, the apostle Paul wrote:

> There is neither Jew nor Gentile, neither slave nor free, nor is there male and female, for you are all one in Christ Jesus.
> *Galatians 3:28*

In a later letter, to the Ephesians, he writes about the collapse of barriers between Jews and Gentiles, who have been together under Jesus in a brand-new category of people:

> For he himself is our peace, who has made the two groups one and has destroyed the barrier, the dividing wall of hostility, by setting aside in his flesh the law with its commands and regulations.

> His purpose was to create in himself one new
> humanity out of the two, thus making peace ...
> *Ephesians 2:14-15*

This is an astonishing vision, a picture which summoned the Ephesian Christians to lay down all of the symbols of ethnic identity and status by which they would have previously defined themselves. While the issue in hand is that of race and religion, the implications of the passage are far greater. As Michael Gorman notes, it seems that:

> Paul would contend that *all* binaries (categories
> built on the splitting of humanity into two groups)
> constructed by humans about humans are
> subverted by the gospel of Christ the peacemaker.[12]

Galatians and Ephesians are not the only Pauline letters where we see this theme emerging. Romans concludes with an exhortation for Jewish and Gentile believers to overcome previous divisions and 'Accept one another, then, just as Christ accepted you' (Romans 15:7). The application of such thinking is economic when the Corinthian Christians are encouraged to see financial equality and the sharing of resources as a response to the generosity of Jesus who gave up His wealth 'so that you through his poverty might become rich' (2 Corinthians 8:9). As we reflect on these letters, it's especially important to remember the situations to which they were first addressed, small communities composed predominantly of the poor in a world which experienced the same divisions between the rich and the other 99 per cent that we do.[13]

This vision of the early church seems far removed from the interaction in the foodbank described earlier. Although some help has been offered, afterwards the volunteer and 'client' each go their separate ways with little sense of the barriers between them having been broken down.

Is there a better way?

In Deuteronomy 8, the people of Israel, on the verge of entry to the Promised Land, are offered an exciting, mouth-watering description of the plenty and prosperity God is about to bestow on them. Their new home will offer a wide range of delicious foods in contrast to the constant diet of manna and quail in the desert. This will be:

> a land where bread will not be scarce and you will
> lack nothing; a land where the rocks are iron and
> you can dig copper out of the hills.
> *Deuteronomy 8:9*

However, amid the promise of greater riches and comfort, there comes a command which points to the dangers and risks that lie ahead:

> You may say to yourself, 'My power and the
> strength of my hands have produced this wealth for
> me.'
> *Deuteronomy 8:17*

The warning provides a reminder of the dangers inherent to wealth, the temptation to think of ourselves as deserving of that which we acquire, to attribute our affluence to our moral superiority and our capacity for industry. Once we have fallen into such a way of thinking, it becomes natural to consider ourselves more 'worthy' or 'together' while consciously or subconsciously passing judgement on those who have less than we do.

What new attitudes or practices can we adopt to help us negotiate some of the dilemmas explored in this chapter? To conclude, I offer three tentative points, each in the form of a question.

Firstly, how might our churches change if we came to understand social action as not only a way of acting, but also a means of being acted upon? Projects such as debt counselling, foodbanks and job clubs are not only opportunities to help others, but they also provide moments when our eyes can be opened, as we come face to face with the struggle and hardship which characterise life for those who are poor. These are opportunities to learn about their skills and experience and also the resilience and resourcefulness needed to survive on a low income, often far greater than those who may waste more and create less because of their relative comfort.

It's now taken as read by most evangelists that an essential practice in modern mission is that of listening, a willingness to hear the perspectives of others before imposing our views upon them. Why should the same principle not apply to social projects? How would we change if we approached our acts of service to our communities not from the starting point of those in the know but as those who need to learn, to have their eyes opened to the realities of life for our neighbours and to their resourcefulness and insights?

It may not always be possible for someone to move house to where their church is located, but they can at least enter into service there with a readiness to learn about the community, what makes it a good place to live in and what problems are experienced by its residents, the structural injustices which consistently prevent people from realising their full potential and the daily dehumanising reality of living with combative or offensive neighbours. But to make such encounters genuinely possible will probably require more than just a rebalancing of how much we speak and how much we listen. It will mean that many of our projects need to be structured in entirely different ways, with a far greater emphasis on values such as participation and freedom of choice. In contrast to the current foodbank model rolled out in so many churches, how might we respond to food poverty in an alternative way? What difference would it make to offer people a choice about what they can eat? Would the process be less of an indignity if there was an opportunity to make a small financial contribution for their food? Would there be more scope for developing relationships if there was no limit on the number of annual visits that people could make?

It also needs to be acknowledged that in order to run projects in this way, the biggest change required is one which would take place in the hearts and minds of volunteers, for whom this new way of working would necessitate a loss of control and a greater vulnerability. Instead of questioning others who come along to our projects, are we willing to place our own attitudes and assumptions under examination?

Secondly, how might the language and terminology we use to share the gospel be rooted more in the experiences and questions of those living on the estates where our churches are located? Bishop Laurie Green has written extensively on ways in which we can encourage what he refers to as 'pavement-level theology',[14] an approach which is driven by the needs and concerns of the poor and derives from a process of exploration where they are empowered to ask questions and think more critically about the structures and circumstances which at present constrain them. Often, we approach evangelism like sales staff with our pitch already worked out: we know what message we will present long before we've known the needs of our audience. But what if we sought to learn a new set of skills, the ability to listen well and then apply the aspects of Jesus' message of hope and liberation which are relevant to the situation we find ourselves in?

Thirdly and finally, how might our attitudes and actions change if we were more self-aware about our wealth, the ways we are diminished by it and its links with a global economic model which sustains the poverty of so many? We need to take time to ask ourselves what, ultimately, we conceive of as the 'good life'? Do we aspire only to be morally upstanding citizens, good producers and consumers, or are we willing to have our view of the world completely renovated by the gospel?

This does not mean that we ought to deny completely the benefits delivered by economic prosperity, but it would require us to set healthy limits on the value we afford it. And it might even prove to be the means of greater liberation, as we're set free from the anxiety and lack of joy which is generated by an endless striving to sustain the lifestyle and image we think is needed to earn the respect of our peers.

How many middle-class members of our churches also feel themselves to be trapped by the demands of their circumstances, looking over their shoulder at the new acquisitions of their neighbours and wondering how they can compete, at the same time buckling under the effects of long hours, mortgage slavery and corporate pressures? When teaching His first followers, Jesus spoke of how 'the pagans run after all these things, and your heavenly Father knows that you need them' (Matthew 6:32). His words seem especially apt for a society like ours, simultaneously more image conscious and more mentally frayed than ever.

Reflecting on these issues, it is difficult to escape the fact so wittily summed up by Woody Allen, that, 'Money is better than poverty, if only for financial reasons.'[15] The daily pressure of wondering where the next meal will come from, of experiencing cold, of desperately considering how an essential household appliance can be repaired or replaced, brings a degree of stress to daily life for the poor which probably cannot be fully understood by those who are better off.[16] While wealth cannot protect the rich from problems such as illness or relationship crises, which almost all people go through, it can be a means of cushioning them at times of need. For example, teenage pregnancy in a middle-class family may be a trauma, but one which can be endured with support and financial resources which keep open the possibility of further education. However, a similarly mistaken choice by someone from a poorer family is likely to have a much greater impact on their life prospects.

Many of us may be familiar with the experience of walking into a new church and seeing a sign in the entrance hall which declares, 'All Welcome'. It's a laudable sentiment, but we will also be aware that in most congregations the issue of welcome will be more complicated, that in the past, issues of sexuality or ethnicity will often have barred entry for some. Many churches are now on a journey of repentance and rediscovery, recognising the justice implications of our previous stances on such issues. Shouldn't the same focus be applied when it comes to welcoming those who are marginalised because of economics? In a society where the gap between the rich and the poor continues to widen, could there be any greater witness to the boundary-breaking, liberating Jesus than local congregations of rich and poor gathering together, sharing what they have with each other and choosing not to define one another on the basis of how they work, what they drive and where they live. To borrow the language of Galatians 3:28, churches where 'there is no longer chav or snob, for all of you are one in Christ Jesus'.

This is a compelling vision, but it's not one which will come without a cost. To take hold of it will require a commitment not just to a congregation but also to the community in which it's located, and also a willingness to understand that the church does not belong to us; nor can we dictate terms to people about the interactions we're willing to have with them. Finally, and perhaps the biggest sacrifice of all, it requires a greater openness on our part, a redrawing of the lines about whom we are willing to listen to and learn from. This could be one way in which our generation of church is being called by Jesus, who told His first followers, 'Whoever finds their life will lose it, and whoever loses their life for my sake will find it' (Matthew 10:39). For early Jewish Christians, there was a cost in worshipping alongside Gentiles, renouncing all they had previously understood about whom God did or didn't accept into His covenant community. There was a price to be paid by slave-owners who sat side by side with those they once regarded as little more than personal property. How many men must have struggled to come to terms with the new Christian community where women were afforded an equal status? These were the radical adjustments made by the early church and part of their radical witness to the watching empire. Are we willing to bridge gaps similar to those they confronted?

For discussion

1. How near to where you live is the church where you worship? How does your proximity to the church affect the way to relate to it?
2. Can you think of ways in which your church's practices, the language it uses and even the layout of its building reflect the preferences of its existing leaders and members? In what ways might they be a barrier to other local people?

3. As we think about how churches relate to those in their local communities, what lessons can we learn from the example of Jesus who was often the guest of others?
4. Do you agree with the suggestion that our efforts to help people can sometimes be ways in which we remain in positions of power over them? Can you think of any examples you've seen of people helping others without taking over?
5. In light of this chapter, can you think of any practical steps your church could take to be more inclusive in its welcome?

Notes

[1] http://religionnews.com/2013/09/27/faithful-end-interview-eugene-peterson/ (accessed 5th July 2019).

[2] Donald McGavran, *Understanding Church Growth* (third edition) (Grand Rapids, MI: Eerdmans,1990), p 209.

[3] See Roy McCloughry, *Men and Masculinity: From Power to Love* (London: Hodder & Stoughton,1992), p 191.

[4] See Ferdinand Mount, *Mind the Gap: The New Class Divide in Britain* (revised edition) (London: Short Books, 2012), p 221.

[5] Zoe Williams, *The Guardian,* 30 March 2015, http://www.theguardian.com/commentisfree/2015/mar/30/seven-moments-general-election-politicians-britain-polls (accessed 5th July 2019).

[6] Quoted in Tim Chester, *Unreached: Growing Churches in Working-Class and Deprived Areas* (Nottingham: IVP, 2012), p 81. Original source, Martyn Lloyd-Jones, *The Christian and the State in Revolutionary Times* (Cambridge: Westminster Conference, 1975), p 103.

[7] Owen Jones, *Chavs: The Demonization of the Working Class* (London: Verso, 2012), pp 1-2.

[8] For a more detailed discussion of these issues, see Chester, *Unreached*, pp 54-56.

[9] See Evangelical Alliance, 'Good News for the Poor? A Snapshot of the Beliefs and Habits of Evangelical Christians in the UK – Summer 2015'.

[10] At the time of writing, July 2019, more than 1,200 foodbanks operate within the UK Trussell Trust network (https://www.trusselltrust.org/news-and-blog/latest-stats/end-year-stats/), while local churches now work with Christians Against Poverty to run 303 CAP Debt Centres and 149 CAP Job Clubs (https://capuk.org/about-us/the-cap-story/cap-services-growth) (both websites accessed 5th July 2019).

[11] See Andy Crouch, *Playing God: Redeeming the Gift of Power* (Downers Grove, IL: IVP, 2013), p 73.

[12] Michael Gorman, *Becoming the Gospel: Paul, Participation, and Mission* (Grand Rapids, MI: Eerdmans, 2015), p 192.

[13] See Bruce Longenecker, *Remember the Poor: Paul, Poverty, and the Greco-Roman World* (Grand Rapids, MI: Eerdmans, 2010), p 45.

[14] See Laurie Green, *Blessed Are the Poor? Urban Poverty and the Church* (London: SCM Press, 2015), p 190.

[15] Ned Sherrin (ed), *The Oxford Dictionary of Humorous Quotations* (Oxford: Oxford University Press, 1995), p 211.

[16] See Linda Tirado, *Hand to Mouth: The Truth about Being Poor in a Wealthy World* (London: Virago, 2014), pp 131-143.

Chapter Five
The Gap between the Abstract and the Concrete

When the story of 2017 is told by historians, one tragic aspect of it will be the terror attacks which brought death and carnage to so many major European cities: the bombing of a concert in Manchester, the shooting of police officers on the Champs-Élysées in Paris, and the deliberate driving of cars or vans into crowds of people in London, Stockholm and Barcelona.

Three days after the Barcelona attack, when thirteen people were killed at La Rambla market, I was on holiday and took the opportunity to worship at another church. The service was uplifting in many ways: it was encouraging to be part of a large gathering of people of many different ages, the worship songs were lively and sung joyfully with arms raised, and the sermon was thoughtful, well delivered and followed by ministry time when several people came forward to express their renewed desire to live with their identity in Christ.

But as the worship songs rolled on, as words of prophecy were shared, as prayers were lifted up, I kept waiting for the prayers to be offered for the victims of

Barcelona. They never came. In fact, the service contained no prayers of intercession, no space in which the needs of the sick or struggling in either the congregation or the wider community could be brought to God. Reflecting on that service a few days later I remembered that moment in *The Muppets*[1] film when Mary, played by Amy Adams, sings about having a 'Me Party'. Except that this occasion could better be described as an 'Us Party': quite a lot of 'us', in fact, and God is also invited along.

Nonetheless, the whole occasion had a sense of being somehow turned it on itself, the focus being on *us* and *our* relationship with the God of love, a vibe of celebration that doesn't want to be disturbed by the painful reality of suffering. Some people may consider this understandable: they may feel that they have to contend with the pressures and challenges of life for the other six days of the week, and they've come to church to get some relief. Given the major political upheavals of recent years, watching the news has often been a stressful business, so escaping the disorder and focusing instead on God may seem like a valid response.

The comedian Mel Brooks once commented:

> Between projects I go into the park and bite the grass and wail, 'Why do you make me aware of the fact that I have to die one day?'
>
> God says, 'Please, I have Chinese people yelling at me, I haven't time for this.'
>
> I say all right, God is like a Jewish waiter, he has too many tables.[2]

And yet, the impression which could be formed from many contemporary church services implies the opposite perspective, a presumption that God might actually be more concerned with the details of our personal lives than the major geo-political events of our day. Aside from the preoccupation with ourselves at the expense of issues such as economic justice or the environment, which take us back into the territory of the individualism explored in Chapter One, we should also acknowledge the lyrical and musical qualities of some worship songs which seem closer to romantic pop ballads than to hymns of old.

Beyond the obvious sense of self-indulgence which comes across in the worst excesses of this 'love-in' approach to worship, isn't there also a case for saying that this sort of devotion is, frankly, a little weird, given that most Christians would hopefully testify that an understanding of God's love for the world was a central tenet of their faith? However, I think it reflects an unspoken but powerful system of categories which operates in many of our churches, a division between the parts of our lives which are relevant to our faith and those which aren't. While recognising that there will be variations in these classifications, depending on which branch of the church we belong to, I suggest a view of the world which runs along the following lines.

God is very interested in	God is quite interested in	God is not interested in
• What happens to me when I die • Whom I am sleeping with • Saying my prayers and reading my Bible	• What I do in work • Whom I am friends with • The amount of food and drink I consume • How I spend my money	• What I do on holiday • The clothes I wear • The car I drive • The TV programmes I watch (provided they're not pornography) • This weekend's football results

Of course, there's an element of tongue-in-cheek in these definitions, but I hope that they also highlight the rather skewed nature of a value system which sometimes breeds a sort of self-obsession about what is personal to us and a certain presumption about the lengths God will go to in order for the world to run in a way convenient to us.

None of this is to deny the loving interest He has in the minor details of our lives. When Jesus reminded the disciples of the attentiveness of God, He spoke of a care that extended to every sparrow that might fall and that caused even the hairs on our heads to be numbered (Matthew 10:29-30). Many of us reading this book will have stories to tell of moments when we have been grateful for what felt to us like the intervention of God in key moments, but is there a line that can be crossed which takes us from dependence on Him to a kind of sanctified navel-gazing?

As a way of unpacking this issue, let's think for a moment about a prayer which many of us will have cried out on more than one occasion: 'Lord, find me a parking space!' I've done it myself, and been grateful when turning the next corner to find a bay waiting for me to drive into. But the more questions we ask about this situation, the more complex it becomes.

If God is sorting out a parking space for me, does that mean He considers my needs more important than others'? After all, didn't Jesus say that God causes the sun to shine and the rain to fall on both the evil and the good (Matthew 5:45)? Are there certain situations which God will intervene in more than others? Is He more likely to find me a parking space when I'm in a hurry for a hospital appointment but less likely if it's my Saturday morning trip to the supermarket? And if I am going to the hospital, does He care more for the people going in for a serious operation or visiting a dying relative than for those who only have a routine check-up? And if God has sorted out a space for me, doesn't that mean He's actually controlled not just my own journey to the hospital or interview, including the timing of traffic lights and the busyness of junctions and roundabouts, but also the almost infinite number of decisions taken and commutes experienced by every other driver who has converged on the same car park at the same time? And finally, and perhaps most importantly of all, why do we consider this to be a situation more worthy of God's interest than others?

Most of us have a tendency to divide our lives between the sacred and the secular, attaching a significance to certain habits related to spiritual devotion and particular aspects of morality (with sex invariably deemed more important than issues of money or power), while thinking of other parts of our lives as somehow off limits to faith. But all of this is a far cry from the view of the world held by those who lived in biblical times. It may come as a surprise to some of us to discover, for example, that classical Hebrew has no actual word which describes what we refer to as 'spirituality', given that Jews in biblical times would have failed to recognise the idea that there are aspects of life which are off limits to God. In their world view, every action and thought of every day took place in the context of their faith in God. Hence the reason why modern Hebrew has had to invent a word for spirituality: *ruchaniyut*.[3] This is an approach to life which understands every moment to be given by God, and every decision to be governed by His rule.

In its most excessive forms, the consequences of this thinking that only some parts of our lives belong to God, with others kept off limits, can be devastating. I've already referred to my experience of growing up in Northern Ireland during the time of the Troubles, and the apparent lack of interest of many churches in peacemaking. Ours was a form of Christianity where what mattered most was 'sound' theology and the sustaining of our personal devotion. We could recite the Five Points of Calvinism, offer a good working definition of penal substitution and we all made sure to have our 'quiet times' each morning, but we didn't know the names of our Catholic neighbours.

How did we get here? How could it be that many of us now live with a perspective which is so far removed from that of our forebears? We've already explored in Chapter One the individualistic emphases which arrived with the advent of evangelicalism, but are there other ways of explaining our tendency to compartmentalise our lives in the ways just discussed?

Keeping it real in a comfortable world

In part, this shift could be explained by the circumstances in which we live, undoubtedly more comfortable and certain than those experienced in ancient times. For the first disciples, Jesus' command to pray for daily bread (Matthew 6:11) would have made sense in a world where this staple food had to be made on a daily basis, with no scope for it to be stored or kept fresh until the following day. For those of us with a comfortable bank balance or a convenience store just around the corner, it is harder to say this prayer with the same sense of conviction. For many people in the ancient world, life was experienced as a daily struggle to get by, supported by subsistence incomes. The notion of a middle class, those who did not regard themselves as rich but who lived in relative comfort with income above and beyond what was needed for essentials, did not exist at this time.[4] The risk of falling into debt was very real for many people (while our natural tendency is to spiritualise some of the parables of Jesus which refer to debt, assuming them to be only about forgiveness, one suspects their original hearers might have considered their meaning to be more literal). The behaviour of the weather could mean the difference between an abundance of food or crop failure and famine, while medical procedures which we regard as routine were far more dangerous. It is understandable, for example, that in a world without painkillers and lacking our present standards of hygiene and sanitation, Paul offered reassurances to women facing the risks of childbirth (1 Timothy 2:15).

This sense of living in a precarious world is reflected in the prayers of the Old Testament. For example, in Psalm 69, David cries out to God for deliverance:

> Rescue me from the mire,
> do not let me sink;
> deliver me from those who hate me,
> from the deep waters.
> Do not let the floodwaters engulf me
> or the depths swallow me up
> or the pit close its mouth over me.
> *Psalm 69:14-15*

For us, a natural reading of this psalm might be one which applies it to the circumstances of our individual lives, thinking of the 'deep waters' as an image which gives expression to the risk of being overwhelmed by personal problems. However, to those who lived in biblical times, the 'sea' was regarded as a place of risk and chaos, a reminder of the disorder and danger which existed in a world where God had not fully brought His will to bear (hence the reason why 'the sea was no more' in

Revelation's culminating vision of the new heaven and the new earth [see Revelation 21:1]). What we find in Psalm 69 is more than a metaphor, and instead a reference to real forces which the ancients believed to affect their daily lives.[5]

These people were not just conscious of spiritual battles. They realised that all of life is tough and were informed in their understanding of it by a faith which explained their own struggles in the context of God's own wrestling with a creation that was not yet fully submitted to His purposes, the God who fought to tame monsters like Behemoth and Leviathan (Job 40:15; 41:1). Although people of faith looked to God for help to survive and wisdom to make the right choices in such a dangerous world, they didn't do so with the expectation of being shielded from problems or misfortune.

It is hard, however, for those of us fortunate enough to be in a position which cushions us from financial pressure, to appreciate this sense of struggle. Instead, much of modern life is experienced as routine, convenient and even humdrum. Week by week we commute to our places of work, while month by month the salaries roll in and the direct debits roll out of our accounts. Of course, people in every time and place have experienced the tedium of performing monotonous tasks, but no generation has had the resources at our disposal to distract us in such moments. At one time we looked to technology to offer us more convenience, yet increasingly it feels as if we use it to relieve our boredom, amusing ourselves with a GIF here, a meme there, ordering some new purchase with 'one click' and then having it arriving the next day.

The sociologist Lynsey Hanley, reflecting on her experience of social mobility, suggests that, 'the middle class approach to life … is founded on a bedrock of security',[6] a confidence in better prospects for the future which justifies planning for the long term and which allows the time and energy needed to think about life in more abstract and conceptual terms. In contrast, she writes:

> the working-class approach to life … embodies generations of uncertainty. For how long can we keep the family together? Will our child survive? Will I still have a job tomorrow?[7]

Once again, we're confronted with the question of how the form of Christianity predominating in many middle-class congregations can answer these questions. Writing in *The Guardian* in August 2013, Abdul Haqq Baker, a convert from Catholicism to Islam, commented on the increasing number of young, mainly black, British men who are choosing to become Muslims. Baker noted:

> The passivity that Christianity promotes is perceived as alien and disconnected to black youths growing up in often violent and challenging urban environments in Britain today. 'Turning the other cheek' invites potential ridicule and abuse whereas resilience, strength and self-dignity evokes respect and, in some cases, fear from unwanted attention.[8]

The immediate response of many of us would probably be to point out how these comments reveal a fundamental misunderstanding of the radical nature of Jesus' instructions in the Sermon on the Mount, where love is shown to enemies in ways which enable victims to subvert the power which their oppressors sustain by violent means. But this perspective is supported by research which suggests that these converts to Islam are drawn to an affirmation of 'masculinity and male comradeship'[9] which is seen to be at odds with a certain form of Christianity perceived as lacking edge when it kicks against the injustice of the world.

In January 2011, *The Independent* reported, 'The number of Britons choosing to become Muslims has nearly doubled in the last decade'.[10] We may be surprised by this figure, given the high social cost of conversion to a religion which has been the subject of suspicion, negative publicity and intense scrutiny, but it suggests that many people in our country are crying out for an expression of faith which is muscular without being dogmatic, which gives moral guidance and discipline, and which provides a strong sense of community and an explanation of all that is wrong in our world while also offering scope for personal change.

The tragedy of this situation lies in our frequent failure to tell our own bigger story. In Mark's Gospel, we find an account of Jesus' ministry which begins with His announcement: 'The kingdom of God has come near. Repent and believe the good news!' (Mark 1:15). This announcement was one of revolution, the arrival of the new reign of God and the eventual ordering of the whole world around His purposes, which followers of Jesus are invited to be part of here and now. How did we get to the point where this wonderful story of hope and liberation has become reduced, in the eyes of many, to a message primarily concerned with individual salvation? How might we recover an understanding of the gospel which is sufficiently robust and expansive that it is able to offer a satisfactory account for the injustice and pain which most of us will experience at one time or another? In the remainder of this chapter, we'll consider three possible approaches which might help us answer this question.

Hearing the call of the kingdom

What would it look like for our churches to present the message of Jesus in a way which emphasises His love for the poor and the specific calling He offers to them and blessing He announces for them (Luke 6:20)? Imagine an invitation which would be more than just a call to give up one's soul to God in the hope of eternal freedom, and which would also offer empowerment in the here and now, the potential to change one's circumstances by breaking out of constraining habits alongside an explanation that sin doesn't manifest itself in our personal failures, but in our experience of the world as a place where bad stuff happens to good people and where the rich and the strong consistently exploit the weak and vulnerable. Imagine also a call for people to take part now in a revolutionary economy and order which are breaking in with the arrival of the kingdom of God.

How would we communicate this message? As we noted earlier, in Chapter Two, in recent years much has been made of the experience of exile and ways in which it might explain the current predicament of the church. But could it be that it's time for the church to stop thinking of this language as belonging only to itself? How might the language of exile offer an expression of the loss experienced by many communities in post-industrial cities and in a globalised world where local businesses are overtaken by seemingly unstoppable economic forces and where local communities are changed by people movements?[11]

In recent years, we've seen a variety of messages delivered to marginalised areas by the political classes. During the New Labour years, the government tended to opt for a tone of technocratic disapproval, investing in communities but doing so with a managerialism which was ready to penalise shiftless or antisocial behaviour, incredibly creating almost one new criminal offence for every day spent in office.[12] In the coalition years, as the government introduced its austerity policies with the aim of reducing the huge deficit created in the wake of the credit crunch, the poor were portrayed as a drain on society, with numerous news headlines and 'poverty porn' journalism designed to foster cynicism and disdain for those dependent on the benefits system. According to *Guardian* journalist Suzanne Moore, the consequence of such portrayals was 'a "gradual erosion of empathy" where poor people "are an entirely different species" and "instead of being disgusted by poverty, we are disgusted by poor people themselves"'.[13] Most recently, the message offered to the 'left behind', in both Britain and the United States, has been that the certainty and predictability of a bygone era can be recovered. We can take back control. America can be made great again.

How can churches offer a different response to the sense of loss and hopelessness felt by so many people? A helpful starting point might be to place more emphasis on Scripture's account of the fallenness of our world and the outrage expressed by the God who longs to 'let justice roll on like a river, righteousness like a never-failing stream' (Amos 5:24). This is the God who has personally involved himself in a battle for liberation, in a mission described in terms of binding a strong man in order to set free those held captive (Luke 11:21-22).

This is a perspective which is helpful in the sense that it refuses to shy away from the reality of evil and the sense of struggle which often characterises life for those who are victims of oppression or injustice. It offers us the vision of a God who is Himself willing to become part of this struggle, entering human experience as part of His mission to bring His order to bear upon a chaotic world. And, accordingly, those who follow Jesus find themselves to be participants in the same struggle, a conflict described in telling terms by the apostle Paul. As we noted in Chapter One, addressing the Ephesians he writes of a struggle:

> against the rulers … the authorities … the powers
> of this dark world and … the spiritual forces of evil
> in the heavenly realms.
> *Ephesians 6:12*

A similar message is delivered to Christians at Corinth, who are told that 'The weapons we fight with are not the weapons of the world' (2 Corinthians 10:4). Elsewhere, a young pastor is encouraged to 'fight the battle well' (1

Timothy 1:18). Meanwhile the same sense of struggle is vividly portrayed in Revelation and its call to encourage a suffering church to persevere and overcome.

Crucially, however, this is not a battle which is fought by conventional military means. The rulers and authorities of the world are not disarmed through coercion; instead the revolution is brought about by Jesus giving Himself up on the cross, and those who follow Him are called to struggle and bear witness in similarly non-violent ways. We don't need to look far to find evidence of the risks of misunderstanding which are inherent in militaristic language, but this shouldn't cause us to shy away from these presentations of the gospel that emphasise the gritty determination of the church to remain faithful to an alternative way of life. We live in a time when 'radical' has become a dirty word, used to speak of our horror and suspicion of those who pursue desperate aims for the sake of other-worldly causes, but we need to be wary of becoming alienated from the experience of the first Christians whose lifestyle marked them out as so different to those around them.

For some of our churches, an important step on this journey will be taking more time to listen to those whose understanding of God has been directly shaped by their experience of struggle, the immigrant communities who have arrived in Britain since the end of the Second World War; those whose experience has been explained by a Black Liberation Theology, described by one writer as a journey from 'nobodies to somebodies'.[14] Their arrival has been a source of renewal for many British churches, but we also need to ask searching questions in light of the racism of some congregations who failed to make room for the *Windrush* generation and those who came after them. How much more could we have learned from those whose ancestors endured the terrible injustices of slavery and who have themselves been on the receiving end of prejudice and racism? How could our worship have been informed by the laments and the spirituals which express pain and the hope of an end to suffering, and how could our pulpits have been changed by the presence of a style of preaching which is passionate, gritty and exhorting? How could the perspectives of this Liberation Theology inform the response we make to those arriving at our foodbanks and debt-counselling services? And how can we make sure we avoid repeating the failures of previous generations at a time when some of the fastest-growing UK churches are those made up of migrants from Eastern Europe and asylum seekers from the Middle East?

Cause and effect

My second reflection on how we might develop an approach to faith which is better able to withstand the rigours and challenges of life is driven, in part, by a pattern I've noticed in conversations which take place in churches in the aftermath of disappointment.

Most of us realise that the life of any congregation will, from time to time, be disrupted by discouragements, that our harmony and confidence will be shaken by a change in someone's behaviour or circumstances. That young Christian who seemed to be making such progress in their faith is no longer attending church. We discover that a marriage is in trouble, even that the problems being experienced by a couple are such that it may not be possible for the relationship to be preserved. Or someone who has been part of the church family for many years begins to drift away, disillusioned, as they are apparently struggling to reconcile their experience of life with the prevailing theology and outlook of the congregation.

Invariably, such moments cause both pain and soul-searching. We look back at what happened and try to figure out if more could have been done to help someone. With hindsight, we discern changing patterns in an individual's behaviour which ought to have alerted us to the danger they were in, if only we had been paying more attention. And we also try to retrospectively come up with solutions which could have prevented this misfortune. 'If only they had made themselves more accountable.' 'If only our church ran marriage or parenting courses.' 'If only that person had been part of a prayer triplet or house group.' We assume that behind every effect there is a cause which could have been prevented by applying an appropriate technique, a perspective which can convey a sense of control and security in God but is found not to be fit for purpose when an illness, an accident or someone else's bad choice collides with our own life in the arbitrary way such events occur.

Often, the solutions which are suggested work on the assumption that most problems can be avoided with the right know-how or routines. So much of what passes for discipleship in our churches is an induction into a right kind of thinking, apparently rooted in the conviction that once our theology is properly aligned, everything else will fall into place. I've attended Christian formation classes which encouraged me to think about my 'identity in Christ' and which instructed me on the right kind of atonement theory to believe in, but without ever addressing issues such as anger management or negotiating disagreements and differences of opinion with other people. This failure to properly attend to our desires, impulses and emotional intelligence and intuition leads to two equally serious risks.

Firstly, we let people down by denying them the possibility to become fully mature and liberated in their faith, meaning they sometimes live for years without facing up to besetting sins and struggles that make them a risk to themselves and others.[15] We have models of discipleship which often seem more effective at teaching theological principles than they are at helping people to deal constructively with difference or to be able to process disappointment without taking out their hurt or lack of self-esteem on others. In each congregation I've attended I've seen behaviour which would be considered sackable in the workplace but which is tolerated by those who insist on the need to 'love people as they are'. I realise the need for our churches to be cultures shaped by grace and long-suffering, but isn't there something sad about the fact that many Christians may stand a better chance of receiving constructive criticism and a 'development plan' in their place of work than in the church they attend? Isn't it a bitter irony that Christians who claim the power of the Holy Spirit to indwell and transform them so often fail to support each other in making meaningful change in their lives?

Often, our failures to become more mature in faith can be the result of a lack of awareness, not just misinformation about the nature of a temptation but, more crucially, an absence of self-understanding. How can discipleship be offered in a way which helps us think more carefully about our impulses and reactions, the reasons why certain circumstances cause us to feel angry or threatened? In what way is our faith journey linked to the stage of life we're at, whether it's the transitions which come with the beginning of marriage and the arrival of a first child or the sense of loss that might arise as we retire or become empty-nesters? If we have a model of church which places a high value on activism and how much we can *do*, how are we preparing people for later seasons in life when failing health or energy levels may not enable us to sustain previous levels of involvement?

Secondly, it's worth questioning the effectiveness of approaches that place the emphasis on belief rather than behaviour. I often hear Christians complain about the need for sermons on 'what we believe' about moral issues, but I wonder how many believers are actually in need of clear instruction on these issues. My guess is that most people who have attended church for many years are clear about the fact it's not good to fiddle their tax return, explode in anger at their colleagues or cheat on their spouse, but that doesn't prevent them from making destructive choices in moments of tension or temptation. I suspect that this is because the 'here's what to believe, go ahead and apply it' approach works better for some people than others... some of us are less inclined to question and more readily willing to comply with a church's party line, and possibly fail to realise that what works for them is failing to satisfy the intellectual curiosity or the impulses and desires of people who are wired differently. Added to this is the fact that the temptations we face are often not based on intellectual conundrums, but have to do instead with physical and material longings. Have you ever wondered why adverts are so full of images of slim, beautiful people and perfectly machined pieces of shiny metal? The marketeers know how we're wired, what visions of alternative ways of looking and acting will appeal to us.

This focus on inputting into the head is probably best evidenced in the format of most gathered worship services on a Sunday. Educational theorists now recognise that there's a wide variety of ways in which people learn most effectively. Some of us find it easier to think in terms of pictures and images than words and definitions. For others, it's more natural to discover and process new ideas in the context of a group discussion. Another approach is often referred to as kinaesthetic and it works most effectively for those who are best informed by the sense of touch. This variety of learning styles is no longer 'new news' to most educational practitioners, and yet most church teaching continues to be delivered in the format of the sermon, a monologue (not always structured with several learning points, creating the effect more of a lecture than a piece of winsome rhetoric) which works best for those who think verbally and are best persuaded by logic and reasoning. Is it any wonder that some people come to think of their faith as somehow remote from the decisions and tasks of everyday life when it's presented to them in a predominantly lofty or cerebral manner?

At this point, we need to acknowledge another strange tension which seems to be played out in many of our churches, the combination of a cerebral approach to ethics alongside the overt emotionalism of many modern worship songs. We've already reflected in this chapter on a pattern of worship familiar to many of us who regularly attend evangelical or charismatic services, most if not all inviting participants to sing of their love for God with intimate language and upbeat melodies. We need to recognise the formative value for many of such services, this weekly experience of worship which provides a sense of encounter which sustains them for the rest of the week when the church is scattered rather than gathered, a perspective recently backed up in academic research. University of Washington researchers have written on the experience of those who attend American megachurches, describing a wave of 'emotional energy' (EE) as they worship, which in turn generates confidence and enthusiasm.[16] The same research indicates that this EE has a 'powerful and motivating effect upon the individual', which could lead to a change in moral behaviour.

These feelings of EE are closely linked to levels of oxytocin, a hormone related to a variety of actions including social recognition and tribal behaviour, including bonding with insiders and the distrust of outsiders (the same kind of buzz experienced by, say, a crowd of football supporters at 3pm on a Saturday afternoon). So far, so good... but what if this experience becomes a kind of addiction, with people returning

Sunday by Sunday in search of the next emotional hit? How can we ensure that this experience doesn't just cause us to look inward, attending only to the needs of our disembodied souls, but asks us to consider issues of justice, politics and the needs of those with whom we will share work, rest and play for the other six days of the week?

There are obvious ways in which our gathered worship can move beyond the abstract to the concrete. Many churches, for example, now make room in their services to reflect on 'this time tomorrow', space for members to talk about the particular challenges and opportunities they face in the week. But perhaps the answer to this question lies less in innovation and more in an embrace of the practices which have been central to Christian worship throughout the church's history. Times of silence and confession ask us, in the presence of God, to examine our motivations and behaviour. Prayers of intercession, especially when attentive to the needs of the wider community and world, also remove us from preoccupation with ourselves. And even though our financial giving is now transacted increasingly by Direct Debit rather than the giving of hard cash into the offering basket, this moment in the service still forces us to consider how generous we are, how much is being returned to God and how much we have withheld. [17]

We might 'feel' that these rituals fail to deliver the emotional high which is offered by newer forms of worship in less traditional churches. But week by week, slowly but surely, they go to work on us. A poignant example of this can be found in the story of the Nickel

Mines tragedy, the dreadful event in October 2006 when a gunman murdered five young girls at an Amish schoolhouse before committing suicide. Afterwards, many people were deeply impressed by the willingness of the Amish community to offer grace and reconciliation towards the family of the killer, Charles Roberts, even going so far as to share some of the money given to victims' families after the tragedy. The Anabaptist historian Steven M Nolt has reflected on the response of the Amish community, citing their commitment to the teachings of Jesus and in particular the understanding that the forgiveness offered to us by God is inextricably linked to the forgiveness we are willing to give others. He writes:

> They immediately point to Jesus' parables on forgiveness and especially to the Lord's Prayer, with its key line: Forgive us as we forgive others.
>
> This phrase rings loudly in Amish ears because they pray the Lord's Prayer frequently. It's not uncommon in the Lancaster, Pennsylvania settlement for Amish people to prayer [sic] the Lord's Prayer eight times a day, and ten times on Sundays. The Amish there discourage composing original prayers and use the Lord's Prayer routinely and liturgically.[18]

Week by week and day by day these words are repeatedly prayed, going to work on the community such that in moments of crisis and testing, forgiveness is a reflex action. If, several times a day, you talk to God about the need to forgive those who have sinned against you, then there's a higher probability that you'll find yourself looking for reconciliation when a relationship is breached, that you'll find yourself refusing to retaliate when faced with some kind of assault.

This touching and profoundly challenging story ought to provoke us to further thought about our worship: the prayers we use, the songs we sing, the subject matter we focus on and that which we consider out of bounds. Jesus did not preach a spirituality which invited people only into relationship with Him. On almost every occasion when He spoke of God's forgiveness, He invariably linked it to our own willingness to be reconciled with the other human beings in our proximity. If themes such as reconciliation, injustice, physical and mental health, the workplace and vocation, family and community relationships are given airtime in our services then we will no longer feel we have been sanctioned to live out our faith with no reference to the everyday.

A songbook for concrete faith: returning to the psalms

What language could help us in our attempts to earth our worship in the concerns of the everyday? What songs could be sung? What prayers could be said? We don't need to look far. A wonderful resource is readily available, 150 songs which give expression to moments of personal joy and lament, cries for reconciliation and pleas for deliverance, as well as marking occasions in the life of a worshipping community.

We've reflected in this chapter on the gap between an idealised, predictable mode of faith and the more disordered messiness of life which can kick against the assumptions forged in the worship arena. It seems to me that we find a similar kind of ironic discord acknowledged within the songbook of Israel. The psalms begin with a text which appears to affirm a black-and-white view of the life of faith:

> Blessed is the one
> who does not walk in step with the wicked
> or stand in the way that sinners take
> or sit in the company of mockers …
> *Psalm 1:1*

Those who follow God, who play by His rules, will be blessed, like the proverbial tree which is consistently fruitful and whose leaves never wither. In comparison, the wicked are swept away 'like chaff' (v4). It's been suggested that this opening poem is the moment in which the psalms are setting out their stall, offering a clear and uncompromising vision and moral conditioning for those being inducted into the way of faith.[19] There can be no room for ambiguity or doubt when such foundations are being established.

And yet most readers will realise that these principles seem to be endlessly undermined in the songs and poems which follow. Time and again the psalms appear to provide us with contradictions of the promises made at their beginning. The righteous are not flourishing, they cry out 'How long … ?', such is their sense of frustration at God's silence (Psalm 13:1). Such moments can drag on interminably. 'My tears have been my food day and night, while people say to me all day long, "Where is your

God?"' (Psalm 42:3) Here is faith which fails to do what it says on the tin. On other occasions we find the psalmist puzzled and perturbed about the apparent success of the wicked, in spite of their determination to live without reference to God: 'For they have no pain; their bodies are sound and sleek. They are not in trouble as others are' (Psalm 73:4-5, NRSV).

These are poems full of contradiction. They affirm a picture of the world where everything works out well for those who trust in God, and as soon as they do so they start to complain about exceptions to the rule. But isn't this how most of us experience life? We seek to hold fast to our beliefs, keeping faith that God is going to be faithful to His promises, but we hold this in tension with our awareness that to be a person of faith means recognising that things will not always work out exactly as we hope. Perhaps it's better to think of Psalm 1 as a proverb more than a promise. A proverb gives advice on what is likely to happen if we proceed in a certain way, but it can't offer a sure guarantee. The early bird won't always catch the worm. Sometimes people will hesitate but it doesn't necessarily follow that they'll lose out as a consequence of doing so.

Of course, this does not mean that we give into despair, or refuse to celebrate. Many of the psalms offer joyful accounts of the good things God is doing for His people in the present, while also reminding them of His great acts in history which help Israel develop a deep memory that can be drawn upon in moments of need. Nonetheless, alongside the hymns of gladness we find songs of lament, refrains which take the experiences of illness, abandonment and defeat and lay them before God with a confidence that He is not insistent on polite or pious language, that nothing is out of bounds in conversation with Him. It is no accident that some of the most famous of these laments concern the experience of exile we have touched upon on several occasions in this book (see, for example, Psalms 44; 74; 137).

What might such a variety of language and themes look like in the context of contemporary worship? Can we imagine a service which offers ample opportunity to speak of the goodness and faithfulness of God, but also provides space for those who presently feel far from Him, which can speak with confidence about His purposes for the world being fulfilled, while crying out on behalf of the present victims of injustice? Biblical lament is not a race to the bottom, a burrowing down to ever-deeper levels of despair. The psalmists frequently speak to God of their fear or pain and invariably a turning point comes, a dawning of greater perspective, in the presence of God and His people, a new hope that God will prevail. It's this sort of 'things are not as they seem moment' which we find in Psalm 73, when the writer, having spoken of the apparent prosperity of the wicked, then realises:

> When I tried to understand all this,
> it troubled me deeply
> till I entered the sanctuary of God;
> then I understood their final destiny.
> *Psalm 73:16-17*

However, for the pain to be healed it must first be announced. As I think back to that service a few days after the La Rambla tragedy, I wonder how many others experienced that dissonance between our worship and the horror of the attack or whatever fears or concerns about their own circumstances were preoccupying them, perhaps even feeling that such anxieties were unworthy of a church service. How can we speak of a God of mercy if our times of worship do not lay before Him all that is broken in our world as well as our loves, all that is crying out for His healing and correction?

It's time for our churches to encourage this kind of 'spirituality', one which understands the remit of faith to extend to every aspect of our lives, which explores the earthy and gritty realities alongside our philosophical questions, and which attends to our day-to-day decisions and behaviours as much as our theoretical concerns.

For discussion

1. Do you agree with the suggestion that we compartmentalise our lives into spiritual and non-spiritual categories? Can you think of practical ways in which we could come to see all of our lives as mattering to God?
2. What is your response to a reading of the Bible which emphasises the idea of conflict and struggle? Is 'radicalisation' something Christians should aspire to?
3. Is it right to suggest that we too readily assume people can be discipled by being taught the right set of techniques? What are the potential benefits and risks from moving away from this sort of thinking?

4. How does the story of the Nickel Mines tragedy and the response of the Amish community challenge the ways habits are (or aren't) formed in your own church setting?
5. How does the worship in your church setting compare with the psalms, their affirmation of confident faith alongside their recognition of the times when our experience doesn't match what's promised? How could you redress the balance, and what would the difference be if you did?

Notes

[1] 2011; Distributed by Walt Disney Studios Motion Pictures.
[2] Quoted in Martin Wroe, *God: What the Critics Say* (London: Hodder & Stoughton, 1992), p 20. Original source unknown.
[3] See Lawrence Kushner, *God Was in This Place & I, I Did Not Know* (25th Anniversary Edition) (Woodstock, VT: Jewish Lights Publishing, 2016), p 29.
[4] See Longenecker, *Remember the Poor,* pp 36-59.
[5] See Gregory Boyd, *The Crucifixion of the Warrior God: Interpreting the Old Testament's Violent Portraits of God in Light of the Cross* (Minneapolis, MN: Fortress Press, 2017), p 1037.
[6] Lynsey Hanley, *Respectable: The Experience of Class* (London: Allen Lane, 2016), p 40.
[7] Hanley, *Respectable,* p 40.
[8] http://www.theguardian.com/commentisfree/2013/aug/19/islam-empower-magnet-black-british-youths (accessed 5th July 2019).
[9] See Richard Reddie, *Black Muslims in Britain* (Oxford: Lion, 2009), p 220.

[10] http://www.independent.co.uk/news/uk/home-news/the-islamification-of-britain-record-numbers-embrace-muslim-faith-2175178.html (accessed 5th July 2019).

[11] See Green, *Blessed Are the Poor*, p 138.

[12] http://www.independent.co.uk/news/uk/politics/blairs-frenzied-law-making-a-new-offence-for-every-day-spent-in-office-412072.html (accessed 5th July 2019).

[13] https://www.theguardian.com/commentisfree/2012/feb/16/suzanne-moore-disgusted-by-poor (accessed 30th July 2019).

[14] See Chris Shannahan, *Voices from the Borderland: Re-imaging Cross-cultural Urban Theology in the Twenty-first Century* (London: Equinox, 2010), pp 139-149.

[15] For a helpful exploration of these issues, see Peter Scazzero, *The Emotionally Healthy Church* (revised edition) (Grand Rapids, MI: Zondervan, 2015).

[16] This research was reported by *Christianity Today* magazine in October 2012, see http://www.christianitytoday.com/ct/2012/october/is-megachurch-worship-addictive.html. The full text of the University of Washington study can be found at: https://www.scribd.com/document/103623517/UW-Megachurch-Study (both accessed 5th July 2019).

[17] For a helpful exploration of these issues, see James K A Smith, *Desiring the Kingdom: Worship, Worldview and Cultural Formation* (Grand Rapids, MI: Baker Academic, 2009), pp 155-214.

[18] https://www.goshen.edu/news/pressarchive/10-02-07-nolt-convo/speech.html (accessed 5th July 2019).

[19] Walter Brueggemann, *The Message of the Psalms: A Theological Commentary* (Minneapolis, MN: Augsburg, 1984), p 39.

Chapter Six
The Gap between the Generations

It's probably a complaint that most of us have heard at some point, or maybe even one which we've made ourselves:

> I see no hope for the future of our people if they are dependent on frivolous youth of today, for certainly all youth are reckless beyond words … When I was young, we were taught to be discreet and respectful of elders, but the present youth are exceedingly disrespectful and impatient of restraint.[1]

If you've ever felt this way yourself, you could be forgiven for assuming that these are the words of one of your contemporaries, perhaps taken from the comment pages of *The Times* or a response written below the line on a blog. But they're actually attributed to Hesiod, a Greek poet who lived in the eighth century BC, and an amusing example of the ways in which the same patterns of miscommunication and frustration between the generations have repeated themselves through history. Elders shake their heads at the shiftlessness and disrespect of the young who, in turn, resent the power and privilege held by an older generation who are wedded to the traditions of the past.

It's helpful to remind ourselves that we are not the first generation of people to experience disconnection and misunderstanding between people of different ages. As we reflect on the differences between the generations and the ways they can affect our churches, we would do well to remember that each one of us is personally implicated in this debate as we go through the cycles of life, from the occasionally callow energy and enthusiasm of youth to the sometimes cynical realism and experience of more advanced years. Most of us will have memories of times when we acted naively in our youth, and will recognise in ourselves famous words which are usually attributed, almost certainly apocryphally, to Mark Twain:

> When I was a boy of fourteen, my father was so ignorant I could hardly stand to have the old man around. But when I got to be twenty-one, I was astonished at how much the old man had learned in seven years.[2]

It's no surprise to discover that the same challenge of tension between the generations appears to have surfaced from time to time in the early church. Peter stresses the command 'you who are younger, submit yourselves to your elders' (1 Peter 5:5). Paul writes to Timothy, encouraging him not to feel cowed as a leader on account of his youth (1 Timothy 4:12), and later reminds him of the need to show respect to people, irrespective of their age:

> Do not rebuke an older man harshly, but exhort him as if he were your father. Treat younger men as brothers, older women as mothers, and younger women as sisters, with absolute purity.
> *1 Timothy 5:1-2*

How many local congregations still offer this sort of opportunity for meaningful relationships to develop between people of different ages? Recent years have seen a significant growth in the number of newer churches who self-consciously reach out to young people, seeking to offer culturally relevant worship and teaching with the goal of raising up a new generation of followers of Jesus. The aim in itself is laudable, but it's hard to shake off a concern about how gifts can be grown in communities where the experience and insights of older people cannot be shared. More importantly, this raises the issue of how effective discipleship can be in a church which is not sharing together the wide range of highs and lows which make up the journey of life. It is a joy for young people to experience a sense of energy and the excitement which comes from relationships being formed and weddings taking place. But is something lost when a community is not sharing moments which come in the later seasons of life, when the loss of health or a loved one may be likely to affect us? In the same way, older, more traditional churches may struggle with illness, bereavements and their declining capacity to serve others without the optimistic perspective and energy brought by those starting out on the journey of life. A healthy church is surely one where there are young people and old people, people with energy and people slowing down, people being born and people dying, people growing stronger and people facing illness.

Once again we find ourselves drawn back to that compelling image of Paul, his vision of the 'new humanity' found in Ephesians 2. The church is to be a place which proclaims to the world the ways in which Jesus has 'broken down the dividing wall, that is, the hostility between us' (Ephesians 2:14, NRSV). As we've already noted, Paul has in his sights the barriers between Jews and Gentiles but he is also making a wider point about the welcome Christ extends to all and the need for the wideness of this mercy to be reflected in diverse churches. At times, this witness will need to take account of specific divisions in a society. A multicultural church is especially needed in a place where there is ethnic division, in the same way that a church of the rich and the poor matters in an economically disadvantaged area. Accordingly, in contemporary Britain, it seems to me that a church of both young and old is more needed than ever. As we noted earlier, the struggle that the young and the old have in understanding each other is as old as humanity itself, but we also need to acknowledge the structural divisions which make this issue an especially urgent one in our time.

The elephant in the room

On 24th June 2016, the United Kingdom awoke to news of an event universally regarded as the most dramatic and important in its post-war era. A majority of 51.9 per cent had voted in favour of withdrawal from the European

Union, a result which exposed sharp divisions in British society. Since the vote, numerous attempts have been made to understand the reasons for Brexit, which has been explained, variously, as a reaction against rising immigration levels, a desire to 'take back control' from foreign bureaucrats, and a revolt against globalisation.

The Brexit result has also been interpreted as one which demonstrates a divergence in attitudes between people of different generations, an unsurprising verdict given the breakdown of how people voted by age. While 71 per cent of eighteen to twenty-four-year-olds voted for Britain to remain in the EU, the likelihood of opting for Leave increased with the age of voters, with 64 per cent of those aged sixty-five or above voting for Brexit.[3]

A number of explanations have been offered for this divergence between these age groups. Some experts suggest that perceptions of being English rather than European increase with age,[4] while others have characterised older generations as obsessively concerned with immigration and a nostalgic desire for a return to a time when Britain was less dependent on foreign partners.[5]

The Brexit result has only added to the resentment that many younger people feel towards the boomer generation, who surfed a wave of post-war prosperity and retired early to live in homes they own and take more holidays that are possible because of their greater spending power.[6] In September 2017, the Resolution Foundation reported, 'Young people in Britain are spending three times more on housing than their grandparents did'.[7] It's little surprise that another survey in the same month revealed that:

> Only 23% thought young people could hope for a better standard of life given concerns about home ownership, job security and retirement finances.[8]

This is not to mention the large amount of debt with which most British students now leave university.

Any reader of the literature which aims to explain the defining characteristics of each age group will quickly learn that deciding when a generation begins and ends, and what it should be called, is a complicated business. For the purposes of this discussion, we'll use the following terminology, which draws on the research of American sociologist Jean Twenge,[9] the British church leadership consultant James Lawrence,[10] and the British apologists and church leaders, Frog and Amy Orr-Ewing.[11]

Who are they?	When were they born?	What are they like?
Baby Boomers	1946-1963	• Beneficiaries of the economic expansion of the 1960s and early 1970s: wider access to university education, affordable housing, improved job opportunities, better food and fitness, the generation who 'never had it so good'.

		• More liberal than previous generations (eg attitudes to abortion, homosexuality, death penalty, civil rights movement, concern for the environment), but growing more conservative in later years. • Other formative experiences: insecurity of the Cold War era, access to the Pill and greater participation of women in workplace, the sexual revolution of the 1960s and 1970s.
Generation X	1964-1983	• More parents working and more parents separating: the 'latchkey kids'. • Pushing back on rules and conformity. • More cynical and eager to deconstruct, suspicious of moral certainties, 'postmodern'. • Perceived as aimless in early adulthood (the *Friends* cohort), now in middle age and working harder than any generation before them.
Millennials	1984-2000	• Sometimes referred to as Generation Y. • Passionate about issues such as social justice, and eager to make a difference.

		• Encouraged to believe in themselves (regarded by some as entitled or overly confident in their own ability), keen on feedback and mentoring. • An expectation of choice, of services which can be personalised to suit their needs, keen on work–life balance. • Often entered adulthood with more fragility, emerging from broken or reconstituted families. Looking for security in their relationships.
iGen	2001 onwards	• The first generation to grow up with no memory of a time without smartphones. • Confident communicating online, but sometimes more wary of face-to-face interaction and less able to empathise with others. • Living at home longer, and facing the prospect of greater student debt and diminished prospects of home ownership. • Inclusive towards people irrespective of gender, religion, race or sexuality. • More cautious (less likely to drink or have sex as teenagers), but possibly less well-equipped for the challenges of adulthood.

As we noted earlier, it's all too easy for each generation to define each other in brushstroke terms, the young regarding their elders as unreconstructed complainants who endlessly compare the present with a better past, while the old bemoan what they think of as the increasing liberalism and self-obsession of the succeeding generations. In each case, there may be an element of truth in the evaluation one group is making of the other, but the situation is more complex than the one suggested by these vague generalisations. As we noted in Chapter One, the reality is that there has been a significant increase in individualism in recent years, but one that takes a different form in each cohort. For Generation X it presented itself as a willingness to deconstruct the assumptions of the past, a group who moved from being 'narcissistic slackers' in their twenties and thirties to grafters in their forties and fifties.[12] This was also the first generation to live their lives fully in the grip of the self-esteem movement. Accordingly, millennials were brought up with an even greater confidence in their ability which sometimes proved harder to reconcile with the realities of the world and the workplace. A complete view of iGen has not yet formed, but for now the picture emerging is one of a generation even more tolerant and inclusive than before, but also struggling to move beyond smartphones and social media to communicate face to face and less confident about what the future holds (not unreasonably, given that they are less likely to find secure employment or buy a home of their own).

These significant differences in experience and outlook are rarely spoken of in our congregations but they manifest themselves in a number of ways, leading to tensions and confusion which need to be brought to the surface to enable many in our churches to understand each other properly.

As I survey the faces and listen to the stories of some of the churches I know, I perceive an increasing divide between two groups of people.

On one side, I see an older generation who can be described as follows:

- They are grieving the decline of many of the churches of which they have been members for most of their lives. Often, this decline is a numerical one, but it also manifests itself in other ways, such as the capacity of a church to maintain the breadth of programmes which existed in the past, for example the loss of Sunday-evening worship services or the closure of certain types of children's work which can either no longer be resourced or which are losing their cultural relevance. Sometimes this sense of loss is compounded by a disappointment in younger people who have neither the time nor the inclination to keep these older ministries going.

- Sometimes such grief expresses itself in a desire to get back to how things were in the past. This might reflect a longing for older practices, but also a harking back to a time when the church seemed to have more status and when life seemed more straightforward, when theology and belief were more fixed and the routines of congregational life more predictable. Such longings are no doubt accentuated by the natural inclination many of us have to remember the past through rose-coloured lenses. For many parents some of the most challenging years are spent with the sleepless nights and seemingly endless demands of looking after babies and toddlers, but years ahead we edit out the memories of our exhaustion and cherish what we regard as a special season in life. In the same way, many in our churches fondly look back on the time when everyone was fitter and could do more and when younger families shared together in watching their children grow.

- In many cases, they may also be the generation who are giving the majority of the money needed to sustain an inherited model of church. Partly this is a reflection of their greater financial resources, but I suspect that it also points to their faithful adherence to disciplines such as tithing and a loyalty to organisations and institutions which is not so prevalent among younger people. This raises an important question about who will pay for church programmes and who will volunteer for leadership when final-salary pensions disappear and when people can no longer retire at an age which leaves open the opportunity for many years of good health and time to serve.

This group differ in several ways from younger generations, about whom the following observations may be made:

- They are equally passionate about service, but their first commitment is often to a cause and not an institution. They care deeply about issues such as justice and equality, and this will lead them to look for churches where they serve in ways which enable them to live out their values, working, for example, to run a foodbank or debt-counselling project. However, they may come to regard the church as a means to this end, hoping it will facilitate their own desire to make a difference but without wanting to support all of the other structures of the institution. These generations want to serve in specific ways, but without the added pressure of attending an evening service or listening to the treasurer's report at a church members' meeting.

- They are confident, sometimes bullishly so, about their ability to lead and are keen to step forward, setting the direction of a church's worship life or its mission activities. From the millennials onwards, younger people have been brought up with a confidence about the difference they can make. Where they feel an older leader is blocking the way, their response may be to withdraw or to take their gifts and abilities to another church where more opportunities are available. This generation will not attach itself to one denominational model: people do not feel the need to always worship in a Baptist or Anglican congregation, they are attracted to churches not because of structure but on the basis of where the energy is or where the Spirit is perceived to be at work.

- This lack of denominational loyalty is sometimes accentuated by the practice of accessing more teaching online and less in the context of gathered worship in the local church, creating the idea of a division between where people learn and where they serve. In the same way, there are more opportunities available to volunteer time and gifts outside the local church, for example, at a night shelter or a mentoring and befriending project. This may suit a younger generation who are used to flexible working hours and accessing services (such as banking and shopping) at a time which is convenient to them, who don't want to be constrained by traditional church programmes when a certain activity has to take place at one time on one night of the week.

- They are under more pressure in their employment and finances, working longer hours than previous generations, often not for the reward of long-term advancement but simply to hold on to a job. In many young families, two parents need to work to earn the level of income required to maintain payments on the average mortgage. Gone are the days when churches could rely on one partner working and freeing up the other to work on its programmes.

For anyone under pressure or dealing with disappointment, it can be difficult to look beyond one's own problems and empathise with the challenges or concerns faced by people in different circumstances. The best starting point for many churches faced with these issues would be a resolve to act more graciously and look more generously upon each other. What would change if the old decided to focus less on youth's lack of institutional commitment and more on its passion for causes? How would the tone of our conversations alter if younger generations made a greater effort to value the loyalty and wisdom of those who have gone before them, resisting the temptation to write off as 'tradition' any note of caution about change?

To do this, however, is only a beginning. It could be argued that the even greater task facing many churches is not to help people understand the challenges of others, but to cultivate a greater self-awareness, an appreciation of what is happening in our hearts as we journey through faith.

The stories of our faith and the stories of our lives

For many, the term 'midlife crisis' is most readily associated with fitness programmes designed to regain youthful vigour, marital temptation or the purchase of a Harley Davidson. People of faith cannot presume to be insulated from such problems. As Joyce Rupp notes:

> The experience of God varies with each person, but many relationships with God take a huge tumble into confusion and emptiness in midlife. Religious beliefs go limp. The God one had known for many years becomes a stranger. The sturdy ground of faith is swept away. There can be long stretches of darkness and feelings of abandonment or disconnection with the divine presence.[13]

Tony Horsfall observes that there are a wide variety of reasons which can lie behind such disorientation.[14] For many, middle age might be a season when we first encounter serious health issues or a significant bereavement, crises which inevitably generate questions about faith which can no longer be satisfactorily answered by the straightforward propositions and frameworks which offered such assurance in our younger years. Others may feel a sense of regret about how much time and energy has been given over to the business of attending meetings and running programmes, boredom and tiredness accentuated by disappointment with the conduct or commitment of others. By middle age, the chances are that most of us will have been through at least one experience of church conflict or the failure of a leader, disappointments which almost inevitably generate feelings of cynicism or ennui. Some respond by walking away from church life, others continue to attend but keep their distance from programmes and activities.

Of course, not everyone will feel this way. There are some people who feel no dissatisfaction from pursuing the same routines and programmes week by week, month by month and year by year. It's the same personalities who are less inclined to doubt and question. I have known some people whose faith has been shaken to the core by loss or illness while others have kept going in such circumstances, apparently without feeling the need to question or reflect in too much depth about what has happened. It is hardly surprising that those who respond differently in such moments find it hard to understand each other's perspectives about wider issues of faith and church life.

The most famous exploration of how faith develops during the course of our lives is probably that proposed by the American psychologist and theologian James Fowler.[15] In light of extensive research and interviews with Jews, Catholics, Protestants, agnostics and atheists, Fowler proposed a framework which sees faith develop in up to six different stages over a lifetime.

For those who come to faith at a young age, the early experience of God will largely be that which has been provided by others, for example when grace is said at mealtimes and when parents talk about church. In these early stages of development, key texts are interpreted in literal terms that encourage black-and-white perspectives on matters of faith, ways for adherents to determine who's right and who's wrong, who's inside the tent and who should be left outside. People's beliefs and values are often grounded in an authority outside themselves, such as a favoured church leader, preacher or writer.

People who grow in their faith turn out to be those who go through a process of unlearning many previously valued beliefs and assumptions. Mature believers are not just concerned with intellectual creeds. They place a higher value on virtues such as consistency and authenticity in others, perhaps because of disappointments in life and a dissatisfaction with what they regard as a lack of integrity in either theological frameworks or the conduct of others in their faith community. These believers are no longer willing to follow the crowd or give unquestioning assent to what the church says they must do or believe and are looking for the freedom to explore ideas for themselves. They value opportunities to question beliefs and give expression to their doubts.

The transition to latter stages of faith is rarely reached before middle age. For some, it comes with a realisation of the reality and impending nearness of death, while for others it is rooted in an even greater awareness of the complexity and mystery of life, a humble recognition of the limits of what can be known with certainty. By now people who have developed greater skills in reflection are no longer troubled by the need to hold apparently contradictory ideas in tension with each other, nor do they feel the need to identify themselves by a theological label. They are also increasingly open to what they can learn from other faith traditions. It's also worth noting that another hallmark of such maturity is that believers no longer feel such a need for the affirmation or approval of others, a change which is liberating for themselves but infuriating to those who place a greater emphasis on more rigid theological frameworks which are used to measure the credentials of others. The ultimate stage of faith is a rare one reached by the few who achieve an almost other-worldly degree of liberation because of their commitment to God.

It's important to note that this is not a one-size-fits-all model. Not everyone progresses from stage to stage at the same speed. In fact, some people may never move beyond the black-and-white perspectives of their earliest beliefs.

One of the key questions which is raised by this model is the reason why some people move through stages of faith, while others become stuck at a certain point in the journey.

Fowler identifies three significant influences. An intense trauma or experience of suffering can provide the prompt for people to reassess their belief and actions, though not necessarily so. As a pastor, I am continually perplexed at how some people learn from their mistakes and experiences while others seem destined to repeat the same mistakes over and over again, apparently unable to reflect on what has gone wrong and decide differently the next time a quandary arises. It is often taken as a given that people become wiser as they get older, but this doesn't happen automatically. Churches which help people grow will be those who offer tools that help people make sense of such patterns and habits in their lives.

In addition, Fowler points to the value of education, providing people with new perspectives and information which will consistently help them expand their thinking. Are churches only offering people the same continued diet of basic gospel messages, or sermons on ethics which never go beyond the predictable subjects of cigarettes, alcohol and sexuality, or are they encouraged to apply the perspectives of Scripture to every aspect of life? It could also be the case that the experience of different generations makes some more open than others to go on the journey mapped out by Fowler. Boomers are ready to question and deconstruct (is it any surprise that this was the generation who gave us the Emergent Church movement?), but their tendency to do so may lead only to a hollowing out of belief. Millennials and iGen are hungry for feedback and mentoring, but who will provide them with a rooted and stable context in which to make their journeys of self-discovery?

While most of us recognise the importance of growth, we also will be aware of the challenges it brings. For the last eighteen years, it has been a joy to see our two children transition through the toddler years to primary and then secondary school, now arriving to adulthood. We have also learned, however, that growing pains come in all shapes and sizes, not just the ache of limbs which are stretching and expanding. Growing is tiring, and dependent on a healthy diet. It requires a constant need for new clothes to fit a larger frame, new material to feed an expanding mind. And for parents who are along for the ride, the process will require them to constantly renegotiate boundaries in relationships. At just the moment we think we have the measure of one phase of their development, the goalposts move again. The parallels with church life seem obvious. Those who are growing in their faith will often present as a disturbance to those behind them on the journey, inconveniencing them with their demand for more space to explore new ideas and disconcerting them with their questioning of long-held assumptions.

When Fowler's model is considered side by side with the differences between the generations considered earlier in this chapter, the challenges of helping the young and the old to understand each other become even more apparent. Our earlier years, when we're younger and have a confidence to lead backed up by energy, may also be the time when we're least able to appreciate the perspectives of others who think differently. Some of those who are older may frustrate us with their apparent unwillingness to try new ideas, but others because they appear to us to lack conviction or seem less ready to impose their views on other people or situations. Conversely, older generations may feel an ambivalence not just about the initiatives suggested by those in their twenties or thirties, but also a wariness rooted in a suspicion of those regarded as lacking the broader perspective which comes with greater experience of life.

Six stages of faith but two halves of life?

Another final and important perspective on the progression of faith during the journey of life is offered by the Franciscan priest, Richard Rohr, who has written insightfully on a spirituality of 'two halves of life'.[16]

The first half of life is a time when we look to establish our sense of self, something we do through such tasks as gaining qualifications, making a home, building a career and starting a family. But it's only later in life that we begin to reflect more seriously on the purpose for which we were created, that deeper sense of calling which gives meaning to our previous striving. Having produced, worked and acquired we now realise that what matters is less the things we possess and more the relationships we have formed and the wisdom we might be able to pass on to others. It's hard to arrive at this point painlessly, yet this doesn't have to mean that the second half is a season of regret or disappointment. An increasing awareness of our limitations can, in fact, bring with it a liberation from the need to achieve or to prove ourselves to others. It is also likely that this release will alter our motivations for service or volunteering. The second half of life is one when we care less about a project reflecting our values and our opinions being rightfully respected, and more a time when we want to give back something of what we have received.

Again, it needs to be acknowledged that not everyone reaches their later years with such a relaxed and generous outlook on life, and that certain people may never actually arrive at such a perspective. Some of us remain so addicted to patterns of buying and selling and planning and progressing that we cannot conceive of any other mode of existence. Think again about all those meetings, all those self-improvement courses, all those projects which offer the satisfaction of always doing, always producing an output but without offering the time and space for something deeper to be formed.

So, how can our churches become places where different generations are drawn closer together, with an appreciation of what each can offer to the other? A starting point might be an attentiveness in worship and preaching to the various changes we all encounter on the journey of life. Most churches, for example, are good at offering encouragement and practical support to young couples when children are born and during the baby and toddler phase. Adjusting to the emotional and physical demands of parenthood can be a hard transition for many couples, but how much attention do we pay to those who are further down the road? In their late teens or early twenties, many children leave their family home and the reality is that their departure will have as dramatic an impact upon their parents as their arrival did, being a time when many feel a sense of grief as they adjust to their new circumstances. Yet this issue is rarely discussed in church, and nor do we talk so much about the transitions of retirement or the increasing pressures which might come as more responsibility is taken on in the workplace. How can more space be created to acknowledge the impact of these changes, the feelings of loss and excitement which they bring, laying it all before God? How might churches help people to understand what is happening during such moments and see each of them as opportunities for growth?

Many churches are effective in bringing together those who are exploring belief or who are new to faith. But could similar spaces be offered for those who have been followers of Jesus but can't remember the last time they were stretched in their thinking about God? How about groups for those who are doubting, for those longing for new perspectives, for those who need help to transition from Critic to Seer? Home groups, the focal point of discipleship in many churches, can be helpful spaces for deepening trust and relationships, but is there a danger that in some, conversation takes place at a lowest common denominator level?

The depth and complexity of the emotions generated by some of these life transitions will be such that even a small group might not be the appropriate context in which to fully explore them. Tony Horsfall has noted the opportunities which are offered by mentoring:

> a form of discipleship which is focused not on a programme but on the needs of the person involved.[17]

We noted earlier what has been described as the 'feedback-hungry' mindset of the Millennials, but surely mentoring has much to offer those beyond just their twenties and thirties. At whatever stage we're at in our journey, questions to ask ourselves, and for churches to help answer, ought to be ones concerning who is speaking into our lives, who has walked before us and knows us well enough to be able to speak wisdom or encouragement into our present circumstances. An older couple or family, for example, could walk with a younger one, and there is no reason why an individual negotiating the challenges of retirement could not be supported for that season by someone who has been through the same experience a few years beforehand. Such a culture could offer enormous potential for personal growth, but it would also require investment on the part of churches who would need to teach people skills which go beyond biblical and theological study. How can we help people to become more effective in processing their own emotions, skilful in listening and gentle in passing their wisdom on to others?

In a recent book on the necessary relearning of conversational skills, the psychologist Sherry Turkle draws upon the wisdom of Rowan Williams:

> For Williams, the empathetic relationship does not begin with 'I know how you feel.' It begins with the realisation that you *don't* know how another feels. In that ignorance, you begin with an offer of conversation: 'Tell me how you feel.' Empathy, for Williams, is an offer of accompaniment and commitment. And making the offer changes you. When you have a growing awareness of how much

you don't know about someone else, you begin to understand how much you don't know about yourself. You learn, says Williams, 'a more demanding kind of attention. You learn patience and a new skill and habit of perspective.'[18]

It is this kind of empathy which is needed in our churches if they are to become places where the generations can properly understand each other, overcoming divisions between themselves and offering hope in a society where the young and the old seem increasingly estranged. The same empathy will need to be learned if we're to effectively bridge the other gaps which have been explored in this book. The questions raised here are complex and quick fixes are not readily available. But this shouldn't deter us from naming the problems at hand and beginning discussions about them. My hope and prayer is that *Bridging the Gaps* can be the means of starting many such conversations.

For discussion

1. Are there any generations which are missing from your church? In what ways are you poorer because of their absence?
2. Do you agree with the observations made here about how younger and older church members relate to each other? What other patterns have you seen?
3. Can you think of ways in which our churches can become places which naturally encourage transitions through the stages of faith suggested by James Fowler?

4. How has your own understanding of God changed as you've got older? Are there aspects of your beliefs which have become more or less important?
5. How do you think the culture of your church would change if more time was invested in the sort of mentoring relationships described at the end of this chapter?

Notes

[1] Quote sourced at: https://medium.com/@saccoallen/i-see-no-hope-for-the-future-of-our-people-if-they-are-dependent-on-frivolous-youth-of-today-for-4660349c0607 (accessed 5th July 2019).

[2] Quote sourced at: https://quoteinvestigator.com/2010/10/10/twain-father/ (accessed 30th July 2019).

[3] Data sourced at: https://yougov.co.uk/news/2016/06/27/how-britain-voted/ (accessed 5th July 2019).

[4] http://www.independent.co.uk/news/uk/politics/brexit-why-did-old-people-vote-leave-young-voters-remain-eu-referendum-a7103996.html (accessed 5th July 2019).

[5] http://uk.businessinsider.com/vince-cable-brexit-was-caused-by-old-voters-obsessed-with-immigration-2017-7 (accessed 5th July 2019).

[6] https://www.theguardian.com/business/2017/sep/29/baby-boomers-are-enjoying-a-second-bite-of-the-economic-cherry (accessed 5th July 2019).

[7] http://www.bbc.co.uk/news/business-41323442 (accessed 5th July 2019).

[8] https://www.theguardian.com/money/2017/sep/09/millennials-wish-they-had-grown-up-in-baby-boomers-times-survey (accessed 5th July 2019).

[9] See Jean Twenge, *iGen* (New York: Atria, 2017), p 7.

[10] See James Lawrence, *Engaging Gen Y: Leading Well across the Generations* (Cambridge: Grove Books, 2012), p 14.

[11] See Amy Orr-Ewing and Frog Orr-Ewing, *Millennials: Reaching and Releasing the Rising Generation* (Beaconsfield: Latimer Minister Press, 2010), pp 13-85. The table is a paraphrase.

[12] http://www.independent.co.uk/life-style/health-and-families/millenials-generation-x-baby-boomers-a7570326.html (accessed 5th July 2019).

[13] Quoted in Tony Horsfall, *Spiritual Growth in a Time of Change: Following God in Midlife* (Abingdon: Bible Reading Fellowship, 2016), p 83. Original source: Joyce Rupp, *Dear Heart Come Home* (New York: Crossroad Publishing, 1996), p 81.

[14] Horsfall, Spiritual Growth in a Time of Change, pp 83-84.

[15] James Fowler, *Stages of Faith: The Psychology of Human Development and the Quest for Meaning* (New York: HarperOne, 1981), pp 122-213. For a helpful application of Fowler's model to Evangelical Christianity, see Alan Jamieson, *A Churchless Faith: Faith Journeys beyond the Churches* (London: SPCK, 2002), pp 108-125.

[16] See Richard Rohr, *Falling Upward: A Spirituality for the Two Halves of Life* (London: SPCK, 2012).

[17] Horsfall, Spiritual Growth in a Time of Change, p 126.

[18] Sherry Turkle, *Reclaiming Conversation: The Power of Talk in a Digital Age* (New York: Penguin Press, 2015), p 172. Quoting from Rowan Williams, 'The Paradoxes of Empathy', Tanner Lectures on Human Values, 8th-10th April 2014.

Bibliography

Abraham, W, *The Logic of Evangelism* (Grand Rapids, MI: Eerdmans, 1989).

Bauckham, R, and Hart, T, *Finding God in the Midst of Life: Old Stories for Contemporary Readers* (Milton Keynes: Paternoster, 2006).

Bebbington, D W, *Evangelicalism in Modern Britain: A History from the 1730s to 1980s* (London: Routledge, 1989).

Bebbington, D W, 'Spurgeon and the Common Man', *Baptist Review of Theology*, Vol 5 No 1, 1995.

Betteridge, A, *Deep Roots, Living Branches: A History of Baptists in the English Western Midlands* (Leicester: Matador, 2010).

Boyd, G, *The Crucifixion of the Warrior God: Interpreting the Old Testament's Violent Portraits of God in Light of the Cross* (Minneapolis, MN: Fortress Press, 2017).

Briggs, A, *Victorian People* (London: Penguin,1955).

Brueggemann, W, *The Message of the Psalms: A Theological Commentary* (Minneapolis, MN: Augsburg, 1984).

Brueggemann, W, *Cadences of Home* (Louisville, KY: Westminster John Knox Press, 1997).

Brueggemann, W, *Out of Babylon* (Nashville, TN: Abingdon, 2010).

Chester, T, *Unreached: Growing Churches in Working-Class and Deprived Areas* (Nottingham: IVP, 2012).

Crompton, T, *Common Cause: The Case for Working with Our Cultural Values* (Godalming: WWF, 2010).

Crouch, A, *Playing God: Redeeming the Gift of Power* (Downers Grove, IL: IVP, 2013).

Elliott, A, and C Lemert, *The New Individualism: The Emotional Costs of Globalisation* (revised edition) (London: Routledge, 2009).

Erre, M, *The Jesus of Suburbia: Have we Tamed the Son of God to Fit Our Lifestyle?* (Nashville, TN: Thomas Nelson, 2006).

Faith in the City: A Call for Action by Church and Nation: The Report of the Archbishop of Canterbury's Commission on Urban Priority Areas (London: Church House Publishing,1985), p 208.

Filby, E, *God and Mrs Thatcher: The Battle for Britain's Soul* (London: Biteback Publishing, 2015).

Fowler, J, *Stages of Faith: The Psychology of Human Development and the Quest for Meaning* (New York: HarperOne, 1981).

Frost, M, *Exiles* (Peabody, MA: Hendrickson, 2006).

Goldingay, J, *Jeremiah for Everyone* (London: SPCK, 2015).

Goodman, M, 'Numerical Decline amongst English Baptists 1930-1939', *Baptist Quarterly*, Vol XXXVI, 1996.

Gorman, M, *Becoming the Gospel: Paul, Participation, and Mission* (Grand Rapids, MI: Eerdmans, 2015).

Green, J, *The New International Commentary on the New Testament: The Gospel of Luke* (Grand Rapids: Eerdmans, 1997).

Green, L, *Blessed Are the Poor? Urban Poverty and the Church* (London: SCM Press, 2015).

Haley Barton, R, *Sacred Rhythms* (Grand Rapids, MI: Zondervan, 2011).

Hanley, L, *Respectable: The Experience of Class* (London: Allen Lane, 2016).

Hattersley, R, *The Catholics* (London: Chatto & Windus, 2017).

Heffernan, M, *Wilful Blindness: Why We Ignore the Obvious at Our Peril* (London: Simon & Schuster, 2011).

Hilton, M, McKay, J, Crowson N and Mouhot, J-F, *The Politics of Expertise: How NGOs Shaped Modern Britain* (Oxford: Oxford University Press, 2013).

Horsfall, T, *Spiritual Growth in a Time of Change: Following God in Midlife* (Abingdon: Bible Reading Fellowship, 2016).

Horton, M, *Ordinary: Sustainable Faith in a Radical, Restless World* (Grand Rapids, MI: Zondervan, 2014).

Jamieson, A, *A Churchless Faith: Faith Journeys beyond the Churches* (London: SPCK, 2002).

Jones, I, *The Local Church and Generational Change in Birmingham 1945-2000* (Woodbridge: Boydell Press, 2012).

Jones, O, *Chavs: The Demonization of the Working Class* (London: Verso, 2012).

Koyama, K, *Three Mile an Hour God* (Maryknoll, NY: Orbis, 1979).

Kushner, L, *God Was in This Place & I, I Did Not Know* (25th anniversary edition) (Woodstock, VT: Jewish Lights Publishing, 2016).

Lawrence, J, *Engaging Gen Y: Leading Well Across the Generations* (Cambridge: Grove Books, 2012).

Longenecker, B, *Remember the Poor: Paul, Poverty, and the Greco-Roman World* (Grand Rapids, MI: Eerdmans, 2010).

McCloughry, R, *Men and Masculinity: From Power to Love* (London: Hodder & Stoughton,1992).

McGavran, D, *Understanding Church Growth* (Third Edition) (Grand Rapids, MI: Eerdmans,1990).

Marr, A, *The Making of Modern Britain* (London: Macmillan, 2009).

Mount, F, *Mind the Gap: The New Class Divide in Britain* (revised edition) (London: Short Books, 2012).

Mulder, M, *Shades of White Flight: Evangelical Congregations and Urban Departure* (New Brunswick, NJ: Rutgers University Press, 2015).

Orr-Ewing, A and Orr-Ewing, F, *Millennials: Reaching and Releasing the Rising Generation* (Beaconsfield: Latimer Minister Press, 2010).

Prochaska, F, *Christianity and Social Service in Modern Britain: The Disinherited Spirit* (Oxford: OUP, 2006).

Reddie, R, *Black Muslims in Britain* (Oxford: Lion, 2009).

Rohr, R, *Falling Upward: A Spirituality for the Two Halves of Life* (London: SPCK, 2012).

Sandbrook, D, *The Great British Dream Factory* (London: Allen Lane, 2015).

Savage, M, *Social Class in the 21st Century* (London: Pelican, 2015).

Scazzero, P, *The Emotionally Healthy Church* (revised edition) (Grand Rapids, MI: Zondervan, 2015).

Shannahan, C, *Voices from the Borderland: Re-imaging Cross-cultural Urban Theology in the Twenty-first Century* (London: Equinox, 2010).

Sherrin N (ed), *The Oxford Dictionary of Humorous Quotations* (Oxford: Oxford University Press, 1995).

Smith, C S, and Pattison, J, *Slow Church: Cultivating Community in the Patient Way of Jesus* (Downers Grove, IL: IVP USA, 2014).

Smith, J K A, *Desiring the Kingdom: Worship, Worldview and Cultural Formation* (Grand Rapids, MI: Baker Academic, 2009).

Snowdon, C, *Closing Time: Who's Killing the British Pub?* (London: Institute of Economic Affairs, 2014).

Stein, R, *The New American Commentary: Luke* (Nashville, TN: Broadman & Holman, 1992).

Tirado, L, *Hand to Mouth: The Truth about Being Poor in a Wealthy World* (London: Virago, 2014).

Turkle, S, *Reclaiming Conversation: The Power of Talk in a Digital Age* (New York: Penguin Press, 2015).

Twenge, J, *iGen* (New York: Atria, 2017).

Worrall, B G, *The Making of the Modern Church: Christianity in England since 1800* (revised edition) (London: SPCK, 1993).

Wroe, M, *God: What the Critics Say* (London: Hodder & Stoughton, 1992).